FOLLOWING
KING JESUS

HOW TO KNOW, READ, LIVE, AND SHOW THE GOSPEL

SCOT MCKNIGHT

AND BECKY CASTLE MILLER

DEDICATION

To the people of Damascus Road International Church.
Continue to follow King Jesus as you love as Jesus loved, teach
what Jesus taught, and obey as Jesus obeyed.

—Becky Castle Miller

ZONDERVAN

Following King Jesus
Copyright © 2019 by Scot McKnight

ISBN 978-0-310-10599-2 (softcover)

ISBN 978-0-310-10600-5 (ebook)

Requests for information should be addressed to:
Zondervan, *3900 Sparks Dr. SE, Grand Rapids, Michigan 49546*

Art direction: studiogearbox.com
Interior design: Kait Lamphere

Printed in the United States of America

19 20 21 22 23 24 25 26 27 28 29 30 /LSC/ 23 22 21 20 19 18 17 16 15 14 13 12 11 10 9 8 7 6 5 4 3 2 1

CONTENTS

Showing the Gospel

INTRODUCTION

By Becky Castle Miller

What is the difference between a Christian and a follower of Jesus?

There shouldn't be one.

But in practice, often there is. We "*Christ*-ians" don't always follow the One whose name we bear. I know, because I've called myself a Christian for thirty-three years, but for long stretches of that time, the religion I practiced had little to do with Jesus.

I inherited Christianity along with brown eyes and big feet. I am a preacher's kid, which gives fair credit to my dad, the preacher, but not enough to my mom, who raised me on Bible stories and prayed with me at bedtime when I was four to "ask Jesus into my heart." I lived in a Missouri parsonage and rode my Big Wheel tricycle on the short path between the back door of the house and the back door of the church. I learned to sing the praise chorus "As the Deer" before I learned "Twinkle, Twinkle, Little Star." Christianity was not a part of my life; it *was* my life. Even though I knew all about Jesus, he got awfully buried under "Christianity" and the rules that went along with it. The Christianity I grew up with tried to keep me safe:

- Believe precisely this way and your doctrine will be safe. (And shun anyone who believes differently because they aren't real Christians.)
- Follow these principles about relationships and your heart will be safe.
- Do these practices and your spiritual life will be safe.
- Stay in your place and the men in authority will keep you safe.
- Keep all these God-ordained rules, and you will have a happy, blessed life and be safe in heaven when you die.

There was only one problem: the rules didn't work. One by one, I found out the promises were false. The rules didn't keep me safe from a broken heart. They didn't keep me safe from abuse. They didn't keep me safe from "Christian" leaders who misused their power. My Christianity crumbled in my twenties when I realized I wasn't safe, and I wasn't happy, and some of the well-known Christian teachers who had made the promises and the rules turned out to be hypocrites I could no longer trust.

I couldn't handle the feeling of my spiritual guts tumbling out, so I held myself together with the rubber bands of willpower and denial. It worked for a few years while I graduated college, got a job, got married, had a couple kids, and half-heartedly volunteered at my church. Not half-hearted because I lacked enthusiasm, but half-hearted because I was so locked up to keep myself from *feeling* anything that I only had half a heart to give.

Postpartum depression and repressed grief and trauma finally stretched all those rubber bands till they snapped, and I fell apart. An emotional breakdown left me crying every day, barely functioning, and fighting for my life against suicidal thoughts. That raw, empty place is where God met me in the wild comfort of the Holy Spirit and set me on a healing journey that transformed not only my mind and my heart but also my spirit. As I healed through therapy and antidepressants, I began deconstructing and reconstructing my Christianity. Through that whole painful process, I learned what Christianity was really about.

It's not about a set of inward beliefs and outward cultural religious practices. It's not about safety, and it's not about rules. It's about being transformed inside and out into knowing, thinking, feeling, acting, and loving like Jesus. In other words, being a Christian is about *actually following Jesus*.

Scot McKnight writes about his transformed thinking on what a Christian is supposed to be in his book *One.Life*:

> The question: *What is a Christian?* . . .
>
> My former answer: *A Christian is someone who has accepted Jesus, and the Christian life focuses on personal practices of piety.*
>
> Now in my third decade of studying and teaching the Gospels, I want to sketch how Jesus understood what we call "the Christian life." If we were to ask Jesus our question—*What is a Christian?*—what would he say? . . . Jesus' answer, which he stated a number of times, was, "Follow me." Or, "Become my disciple." (Page 15)

Jesus is disruptive—he burst onto the scene bringing chaotic joy into organized religion. Jesus is weird—he healed a blind man by smearing mud on the guy's eyes. Jesus is dangerous—he and many of his disciples got themselves beaten and killed. It turns out that Jesus never promised to keep us safe through rules. He even warned that we would have trouble, that following him was risky to comfortable lives. What he did promise was that he would be *with us* in the suffering. And that promise is one I've found to be true.

Six years ago, I accepted an invitation to move with my family to the Netherlands to serve at an international church. Growing with disciples from all over the world has taught me that following Jesus can look like seven billion different things. You can be Indian and follow Jesus.

Or British. Or Nigerian. Or Chinese. You can be Catholic or Anglican or Protestant or Orthodox, Pentecostal or Liturgical (or any of these). I've seen it all in my church. Whatever style our following Jesus takes, there are only two rules: love God and love people. And we best learn how to live that out together with others in the church.

A few years ago, our pastor took us through "The Jesus Life Challenge." We read one of the gospel accounts of Jesus' life each month for a year, cycling through the four Gospels three times. Spending so much time immersed in the life of Jesus changed *my* life. It helped me continue peeling off the layers of culture and tradition and *rules* that the Christianity of my growing-up years had slapped on top of Jesus himself, and I learned to better orient my Christian life around what Jesus actually taught and did.

As I worked to influence the spiritual formation of my church through Bible study groups, I saw the gaps in our people's discipleship process—and in my own. I read and researched about discipleship and tried multiple approaches to helping people become and grow as students of Jesus. Being re-discipled in this global fellowship of Jesus followers has shown me that it all comes down to this: discipleship is—Christianity is—*Following King Jesus.*

As I've studied with Scot for the past two years at Northern Seminary, I've grown as an academic theologian, but more importantly, I've grown as a follower of Jesus. Scot follows Jesus—this is evident in the ways Scot's scholarship, his ministry, his relationships, and his everyday life are guided by Jesus. In many ways, my conversion story is similar to Scot's. (You can read his story in the introduction to the "Living the Gospel" lessons.) We both grew up in church, both struggled under the weight of legalism, and both found freedom in actually becoming followers of Jesus. I don't ever again want to think I can be an adherent to the religion of Christianity without being a daily apprentice of the Christ.

I've passed on my brown eyes to two of my five children, and my oldest already has feet as big as mine (and steals my shoes). I hope I'm passing Jesus on to them too, in all his complexity and simplicity. Yesterday I was walking with my four-year-old, and we passed a giant crucifix, and she started talking about Jesus and God. I began trying to explain Trinitarian theology, but she interrupted me. "I really want to *see* Jesus," she said.

I got a lump in my throat. "So do I." I can't wait to see him face to face.

I don't know where you are in your understanding of Jesus and in your journey of becoming like him. Maybe you are totally new to believing in and following Jesus. Or maybe you've been a Christian for a long time, but you want to be re-discipled in the ways of Jesus, better shaping your life after his. Whatever your starting point, we invite you to spend the next twenty-four weeks with us learning more about what it means to follow King Jesus and to begin putting that into practice.

HOW TO USE THIS WORKBOOK

This workbook is made up of four sections that address core ideas in the life of following Jesus. The major themes are taken from Scot's books, in this order:

- Knowing the Gospel (*The King Jesus Gospel*)
- Reading the Gospel (*The Blue Parakeet*, second edition)
- Living the Gospel (*One.Life*)
- Showing the Gospel (*A Fellowship of Differents*)

Each of the four sections has six lessons. Each lesson is divided into *Personal Study* and *Group Discussion*. You'll spend time on your own throughout each week reading an excerpt from one of Scot's books (abbreviations used are: KJG in Part 1, BP in Part 2, OL in Part 3, and FOD in Part 4; next you'll read passages from the Bible and answer questions to help you study, pray, and act on what you're learning; and finally you'll reflect by journaling. Then you'll get together with a small group of other people to discuss what you're learning, to do activities to help you interact with these ideas, and to pray for each other. Before you move on to the next lesson, you'll take time to rest.

Here's a little more information about some of the aspects of this workbook.

JESUS CREED

When someone asked Jesus what was the greatest commandment, he said it was to love God, and he added that the second greatest commandment was to love other people. Scot calls this statement "the Jesus Creed." He wrote a book by that name in 2004, and it's also the name of his blog. This is what Scot says about the Jesus Creed:

I began a practice of beginning and ending each day by saying the Jesus Creed. Then I made myself a promise that I'd say the Jesus Creed every time it came to mind, even if it came to mind fifty times per day (which sometimes it has). What happened to me is that I became much more conscious of the need to be more loving. Believe me when I say this is dangerous to your moral health, because it calls into question both our attitudes and practices.

My proposal to you if you want to be a follower of Jesus is to begin and end each day by saying the Jesus Creed, and then say it whenever it comes to mind . . . and then watch what happens to your life. (Page 53, OL)

Scot opens each one of his seminary classes by having all the students say the Jesus Creed together with him: "Hear, O Israel, the Lord our God, the Lord is one. Love the Lord your God with all your heart, with all your soul, with all your mind, and with all your strength. The second is this: love your neighbor as yourself. There is no commandment greater than these." Repeating the priorities of Jesus to ourselves helps us make them our own priorities. In each lesson and each group meeting, you'll say the Jesus Creed out loud—if it feels a little silly at first, keep going anyway. You might become like me and many of his other students who now feel like class hasn't really started until we say the Jesus Creed. May these words sink deep into your heart, soul, mind, and body.

PRAYER

Jesus taught his disciples how to pray by giving them this model prayer:

Our Father in heaven, hallowed be your name, your kingdom come, your will be done, on earth as it is in heaven. Give us today our daily bread. And forgive us our debts, as we also have forgiven our debtors. And lead us not into temptation, but deliver us from the evil one*, for yours is the kingdom and the power and the glory forever. Amen. (Matthew 6:9–13)

Praying like Jesus is one way we can shape our lives to be like his life. In every lesson in this book, you will conclude your prayer time with this prayer, which is often called the Lord's Prayer or the Our Father.

REFLECTION

Processing your thoughts and ideas by writing them down can help you figure out what you think on a topic. Each lesson in this book will give you a prompt for journaling to help you

---

* Or from *evil*; some later manuscripts *one,/ for yours is the kingdom and the power and the glory forever. Amen.*

clarify what you are learning. These entries may also give you a useful tool to map your growth and progress. Hopefully you will see your ideas evolve over the weeks of this study, and you'll notice how Jesus is shaping your mind and heart.

SMALL GROUP

If you are doing this study with a church, your church may have already set you up with a group facilitator, host, and other group members. If you are doing this on your own or with a group of friends, think about the logistics of your group. How many members will you have? Six people might be a good number, though you could meet with two to four or even eight to twelve. A smaller group might get to have deeper discussions but can make it harder to have enough people to consistently meet every week. A larger group may have more lively discussions but will likely have longer meetings! Decide who will facilitate the conversations, who will host your group, and when will you meet. For the facilitators, there is an appendix with tips on leading a small group to help you prepare. (Important: read through the group discussion guide *before* your meeting. Some of the weeks have several activities to choose between or supplies you'll want to prepare.)

REST

Pursuing holistic health for spirit, mind, and body includes rest. Each lesson concludes with a different exercise or approach to help you learn how to incorporate rest into your discipleship.

PART 1

KNOWING THE GOSPEL

Our pastor doesn't really preach the gospel very often," said a well-intentioned woman in my church.

I squinted at her over my mug. "He just spent the entire year going through the Gospels, looking at the story of Jesus and encouraging us to be like Jesus."

"But he doesn't really tell people how to be saved!"

Ah, I realized what she was saying. "You mean he doesn't give *altar calls* very often?"

"Yeah! He doesn't preach the gospel."

I sipped my coffee to hide my smile. A few years before, I might have said the same things as my friend.

I thought of our church's motto that we repeat together every Sunday: *We the church, as followers of Jesus, will love as Jesus loved, teach what Jesus taught, and obey as Jesus obeyed.* I've never been in a more gospel-centered church, and it has changed me.

I said, "I think Pastor Matt is more focused on helping people count the cost of following Jesus and become long-term disciples than he is on making an emotional appeal for a momentary decision."

Is "the gospel" an altar call? Is it telling people how to pray a prayer to "get saved"? Is it a persuasive pitch that addresses an individual's sin by offering them individual forgiveness and an individual ticket to heaven? When I was growing up in church and learning about the Christian faith, I would have said yes. I thought "gospel" meant a message about sin as the sickness and Jesus as the cure, so "evangelism" meant convincing people to accept that message and convert to Christianity.

I'm a big fan of the British TV show *Doctor Who.* The Doctor is an alien from the planet Gallifrey who travels through time and space saving the day in a vessel called the T.A.R.D.I.S. On the outside, it looks like a 1960s police call box, about the size and shape of a red British phone booth, but blue. The Doctor sometimes travels with human companions, and it's a running gag in the show for a new companion to creak open the T.A.R.D.I.S. door and discover a massive spaceship control room—so much larger than the small exterior! Hallways lead off to a labyrinth of passageways and other rooms, including a swimming pool. The humans almost always express their shock by saying, "It's bigger on the inside!" (Though one said, "It's smaller on the outside!")

As I have become more serious about studying theology and growing as a disciple of Jesus, I feel like I'm opening the door of the gospel and gasping, overwhelmed at the beauty and wonder and limitless places to explore—"It's so much bigger on the inside!" I'm learning that "gospel" is more comprehensive, more incredible, and more all-encompassing than a short, individualistic message leading to a one-time decision. The gospel is the whole story of God and God's people, the story that goes from first creation to new creation and hinges in the middle on the incarnation of Jesus and his life and work and teaching and death and resurrection and ascension. The gospel is an invitation to be a part of God's work in remaking the entire cosmos.

The conflation of "gospel" with "personal salvation decision" is pervasive, and it limits the gospel. It misses the point of the gospel Jesus taught. Throughout Galilee and in all the towns and villages he visited, Jesus proclaimed the Good News about the kingdom. The good news is the kingdom news, and the kingdom news is good. There is no gospel apart from the kingdom of God, and there is no gospel apart from the King.

If "preaching the gospel" or "gospeling" simply means asking for a one-time verbal agreement with a set of beliefs about personal salvation, I am no longer interested in doing it. I've seen that message fill churches with people who do not live like subjects of the kingdom, like followers of King Jesus. But if gospeling means telling the story of Jesus, the King of God's people, who are gathered into God's present and future kingdom, then I am excited to proclaim it, to teach what Jesus taught.

> Most of evangelism today is obsessed with getting someone to make a *decision*; the apostles, however, were obsessed with making *disciples*. Those two words—decision and disciples—are behind this entire book. Evangelism that focuses on decisions short circuits . . . the design of the gospel, while evangelism that aims at disciples slows down to offer the full gospel of Jesus and the apostles. (Page 18, KJG)
>
> I believe the word *gospel* has been hijacked by what we believe about personal salvation, and the gospel itself has been reshaped to facilitate making "decisions." The result of this hijacking is that "gospel" no longer means in our world what it originally meant to either Jesus or the apostles. (Page 26, KJG)

This section of the workbook looks at what "gospel" meant to Jesus and Paul and Peter, to help us reclaim a biblical understanding of gospel for today. And as we understand it better, we can share that good news by "gospeling" and creating a gospel culture.

One important point before we begin: *the Gospels* are the four first books of the New Testament—Matthew, Mark, Luke, and John—and they are written records of the life and teachings of Jesus that could be considered memoirs of the apostles or biographies of Jesus. *The gospel* is a message of good news from God—what exactly that message involves is the focus of these lessons. They will also touch on the ways that the Gospels and the gospel interact.

WHAT IS THE GOSPEL?

Learning intent: Disciples will learn a short and clear definition of the gospel: *The Story of Jesus as the resolution of Israel's Story.*

Spiritual formation intent: Disciples will experience all the aspects of this workbook's approach to discipleship and will practice reading, studying the Bible, journaling, praying, spending time with their small group, and resting as facets of growing as followers of Jesus.

▪ PERSONAL STUDY ▪

READING

As you begin your discipleship time today, say the Jesus Creed out loud:

Hear, O Israel, the Lord our God, the Lord is one. Love the Lord your God with all your heart, with all your soul, with all your mind, and with all your strength. The second is this: love your neighbor as yourself. There is no commandment greater than these.

Pre-reading question

1. What is "the gospel"? How would you explain it in one or two sentences to someone who has never heard this word?

What is the gospel?

You may be surprised. You may think the word *gospel*, a word used in the ancient world for declaring good news about something (like a wedding) but used today for our Christian message, is the one thing we *do* understand. You may think that's the one thing around which there is no fog at all. You may think the gospel is the simple thing, whereas everything else—like politics and eschatology and atonement theory and poverty—cries out for debate. Those issues need to be debated, but we really cannot debate them in a Christian manner until we get the gospel question resolved. I think we've got the gospel wrong, or at least our current understanding is only a pale reflection of the gospel of Jesus and the apostles. We need to go back to the Bible to find the original gospel. (Pages 23–24, KJG)

What the Gospel Is Not

In a recent and very rapid email exchange with Pastor Eric about the meaning of the gospel, I stated that each of the Gospels of the New Testament was the gospel itself. Pastor Eric was not so sure.

. . . He said to me, "The gospel is about our sins, Jesus as our Savior, and our need to believe by accepting him into our heart."

I pushed back again: Did Jesus preach this gospel?

His response shocked me: "No, Jesus didn't preach this gospel." Before I could say another word, he sent me another email: "The gospel is not about Jesus as Lord, about being a disciple of Jesus, about the kingdom vision for social justice and changing the world. It's about three things: admitting you're a sinner, understanding Jesus as the Savior on the cross, and believing in that by consciously accepting him as Savior . . . the gospel is about grace so anyone who pushes for kingdom, repentance, and following Jesus is pushing into the realm of works."

Pastor Eric wants to preach an understandable gospel for all people, and he has been very successful at leading folks to Christ, but he has often (he later admitted to me over the phone) struggled with so many who "accept" Christ but don't "obey" him. That struggle is in part created by his "salvation culture" gospel.

We will argue in this book that the apostolic gospel, because it is a gospel culture gospel and not a salvation culture gospel, did not have this struggle. This struggle is our own making. You can play with the words all you want, but that kind of salvation culture gospel will always create the problem of discipleship.

. . . the gospel of Jesus and that of the apostles, both of which created a *gospel* culture and not simply a salvation culture, was a gospel that carried within it the power, the capacity, and the requirement to summon people who wanted to be "in" to be The Discipled. (Pages 32–33, KJG)

What the Gospel Is

> The *Story of Israel*, or the Bible, is the sweep of how the Bible's plot unfolds: the creation of the world as God's temple, the placing of two little Eikons—Adam and Eve as divine image-bearers—in the garden temple of God (called Eden) to represent God, to govern for God, and to relate to God, self, others, and the world in a redemptive way. The single task of representing God and governing God's garden was radically distorted when Adam and Eve rebelled against the good command of God. God banished them from Eden. We can't skip now to Jesus and to the New Testament and think we understand the Story of Israel/the Bible. The Bible, page after page, takes another path. . . .
>
> God chose one person, Abraham, and then through him one people, Israel, and then later the Church, to be God's priests and rulers in this world on God's behalf. What Adam was to do in the Garden—that is, to govern this world redemptively on God's behalf—is the mission God gives to Israel. Like Adam, Israel failed, and so did its kings. So God sent his Son to do what Adam and Israel and the kings did not (and evidently could not) do and to rescue everyone from their sins and systemic evil and Satan (the adversary). Hence, the Son is the one who rules as Messiah and Lord.
>
> Notice this: what God does in sending the Son is to establish Jesus as the Messiah, which means King, and God established in Jesus Christ the kingdom of God, which means the King is ruling in his kingdom. We need to restate this: the idea of King and kingdom are connected to the original creation. God wanted the Eikons, Adam and Eve, to rule in this world. They failed, so God sent his Son to rule. As its King and Messiah and Lord, the Son commissions the Church to bear witness to the world of the redemption in Jesus Christ, the true King, and to embody the kingdom as the people of God.
>
> The Story of Jesus brings the Story of Israel to its *telos* point, to its fulfillment, to its completion, or to its resolution. (Pages 35–36, KJG)
>
> The Story of Jesus is about his kingdom vision, and this kingdom vision emerges out of the creation story, out of Israel's Story of trying to live out God's design for Israel . . . (Page 37, KJG)
>
> [The gospel is] the Story of Jesus as the resolution of Israel's Story. (Page 44, KJG)

Reflection questions on the reading

1. Look back at your answer to the pre-reading question and see how you previously defined the gospel. After completing the reading, how would you define the gospel differently?

2. From the reading above, how would you summarize what the gospel is NOT?

3. Based on your own thoughts and experiences, what else might you add to what the gospel is NOT?

4. Try writing the Story of Israel, as outlined in the reading, in two or three sentences:

BIBLE STUDY

Jesus' Mission Statement (Luke 4)

Luke tells the story of Jesus beginning his public ministry after his baptism and preparation time in the desert. Jesus showed up in his hometown synagogue and read from the sacred scrolls a passage from the prophet Isaiah. This could be considered Jesus' own announcement of the "mission statement" for his work that he was about to start.

Read Luke 4:14–21.

1. Try to imagine Jesus' family and friends listening to him and watching him make this declaration. How might they have felt?

2. How do you think Jesus might have felt as he stood in front of his family and friends and proclaimed his identity, his calling, and his work?

3. Jesus said this prophecy was being fulfilled in their hearing, implying that he was the one who was doing these works Isaiah had prophesied. What actions did the Scripture foretell? List them here.

4. Based on what you know about Jesus, which of those actions you listed above did he accomplish? If you want to take more time on your Bible study, look for sections in the Gospels where Jesus did these various works.

5. The goal of a disciple is to become like her or his teacher. If we are followers of Jesus, what kinds of actions should define our lives?

PRAYER

Prayer shapes us, and praying like Jesus prayed can shape us to be like him. Try reading the Lord's Prayer out loud several times, putting emphasis on different words and sentences each time. What do you learn about Jesus from looking at his example of prayer?

Our Father in heaven, hallowed be your name, your kingdom come, your will be done, on earth as it is in heaven. Give us today our daily bread. And forgive us our debts, as we also have forgiven our debtors. And lead us not into temptation, but deliver us from the evil one, for yours is the kingdom and the power and the glory forever. Amen.

ACTION

Both in his ministry "mission statement" in Luke 4 and throughout his ministry, Jesus focused on people who were poor, people who were imprisoned, people who were blind or suffering other physical ailments, and people who were oppressed.

▓ Think of a person or people group you know, or at least know about, for each of those categories. Write their names or group identities here:

Poor:

Imprisoned:

Blind/sick:

Oppressed:

▓ How would Jesus see each of those people or groups? What would he do for them?

REFLECTION

▓ Begin your journaling process by writing down what you hope to learn through this study. Why are you doing this? What questions do you have about following King Jesus? What do you want to gain during this process? Set a timer for ten minutes and try to keep writing continuously, not worrying about your neatness or spelling or grammar.

■ GROUP DISCUSSION ■

When your group meeting begins, say the Jesus Creed together:

Hear, O Israel, the Lord our God, the Lord is one. Love the Lord your God with all your heart, with all your soul, with all your mind, and with all your strength. The second is this: love your neighbor as yourself. There is no commandment greater than these.

The following questions are based on the personal study you already have completed. Monitor how much time your group has for discussion and answer as many of these questions together as you can.

INTRODUCTION

As this is likely your first meeting together as a group, spend time at the start getting to know each other. Introduce yourselves and share a little about your life and where you are in following King Jesus. Would you consider yourself a Christian? Or are you simply curious to know more about Jesus? Share the stories of your spiritual journeys with each other.

If your group does not already have a facilitator, choose one person to facilitate the group. Or, those who are willing to facilitate could take turns each week reading out the questions and guiding the conversation. Discuss any group logistics that still need to be figured out. Where and when will you meet? How long will your meetings last? Will you share a meal or snacks together? Discuss your expectations for confidentiality: as you share personal information with each other, do you want to make sure that the group members commit to keeping that information only among each other?

READING

▨ How did you define the gospel before the reading?

▨ How did you define the gospel after the reading?

When have you heard a pastor explain the gospel like Pastor Eric did? What did you think at the time, and what do you think about that explanation now?

What did you agree with in the reading?

What did you disagree with in the reading?

BIBLE STUDY

As you tried to imagine the thoughts and feelings of Jesus and his family and friends in the synagogue scene, what ideas came to mind about this moment?

What do you think about viewing Luke 4 as Jesus' mission statement for his ministry? Explain why you do or do not think that is an accurate perspective.

What does this passage reveal to you about Jesus' priorities?

What are other Gospel passages you would use instead of or in addition to this one to show Jesus' vision or goal for his ministry?

PRAYER

■ Did you grow up in a Christian tradition that regularly prayed the Lord's Prayer? If yes, what was your experience with that?

■ What do you think about praying a scripted prayer like this?

■ As you read the prayer out loud, putting emphasis on different parts, what did you learn or discover?

■ Did this feel like praying to you, or did it feel like reading?

ACTION

■ Which people or people groups did you list for each of the categories Jesus spoke about in Luke 4? If you named specific individuals and you think they would not like their names shared, you may keep those to yourself.

■ What do you think Jesus would say to or do for the people you listed?

■ How have you spoken about or spoken to the people you listed?

REFLECTION

Let each group member share their goals for doing this study. (If you have already covered this in your introduction time, you can skip it here.) What do you hope to gain from the personal study time? What do you expect from the small group time?

GROUP PRAYER

Share briefly about your experiences with group prayer in the past, if you have any. Do you feel comfortable praying out loud? Do you mind having others pray for you? Are you okay with holding hands or someone placing a hand on your shoulder or arm?

Anyone who would like to can conclude your first session together by praying a closing prayer, asking God to guide and teach you through this study.

As your group meeting ends, pray the Lord's Prayer together.

Our Father in heaven, hallowed be your name, your kingdom come, your will be done, on earth as it is in heaven. Give us today our daily bread. And forgive us our debts, as we also have forgiven our debtors. And lead us not into temptation, but deliver us from the evil one, for yours is the kingdom and the power and the glory forever. Amen. (Matthew 6:9–13)

REST

After your first week of study, take a day off and do something you enjoy.

2

LESSON 2

THE APOSTOLIC GOSPEL OF PAUL

Learning intent: Disciples will learn the first gospel message that was passed down from the apostles.

Spiritual formation intent: Disciples will shape their view of the gospel according to the apostolic tradition and begin passing on that message to others.

■ PERSONAL STUDY ■

READING PART 1

As you begin your discipleship time today, say the Jesus Creed out loud:

Hear, O Israel, the Lord our God, the Lord is one. Love the Lord your God with all your heart, with all your soul, with all your mind, and with all your strength. The second is this: love your neighbor as yourself. There is no commandment greater than these.

The best place to begin is the *one place in the entire New Testament where someone actually comes close to defining the word* gospel. First Corinthians 15 is that place.

One of the biggest advantages of this one-of-a-kind definition of the gospel is that many scholars think it is also among the "oldest" set of lines in the entire New Testament. Scholars think this was the oral tradition about the gospel that every New Testament apostle received and then passed on. First Corinthians 15 is nothing less than a lifting up of the curtains in the earliest days of the church; it tells us what everyone believed and what everyone preached. This passage is the *apostolic gospel tradition.* Thus . . .

> Before there was a New Testament . . .
>
> Before the apostles were beginning to write letters . . .
>
> Before the Gospels were written . . .
>
> There was the gospel.
>
> *In the beginning was the gospel.*
>
> That gospel is now found in 1 Corinthians 15. (Page 46, KJG)
>
> It will be useful for what follows to break Paul's words into three parts: A, B, and C. Part A is the introduction, and Part B defines the gospel. But because many think 15:20–28, after more than a dozen verses of interruption, continues Paul's "gospel statement," I'll include [those verses] too as Part C. . . . This is where Paul began, and it is where we will begin. (Page 47, KJG)

BIBLE STUDY

Because this Bible passage is central to Scot's points in the reading, it's important to pause here and study the Bible. The next reading section in this lesson will then expound on the Bible study.

Paul's Gospel (1 Corinthians 15)

> This definition of "gospel" by the apostle Paul is the place to begin, and if we begin here, we will find both the meaning of "gospel" and we will have a map that will show how to navigate the rest of the New Testament and church history! If we begin here, we take the first step in creating a gospel culture. (Page 48, KJG)

Read 1 Corinthians 15:1–2.

1. Copy the text of the first two verses here. Writing Scripture by hand can be a good way to slow down and consider it word by word as well as engage hands and eyes and mind together.

2. What did the Corinthian believers do after Paul preached the gospel to them?

3. How does Paul link "gospel" and "salvation" in these verses?

Read 1 Corinthians 15:3–5.

1. Copy the text of verses 3, 4, and 5 here.

2. What four things did Paul pass on to them, that he considered most important?

3. What phrase does Paul use twice in these verses?

Read 1 Corinthians 15:20–28.

1. What does Paul say about the kingdom in these verses?

2. Who will reign?

3. What do these verses say about the victory of Jesus? What is the last enemy to be destroyed?

READING PART 2

The authentic apostolic gospel, the gospel Paul received and passed on and the one the Corinthians received, concerns these events in the life of Jesus:

that Christ died,

that Christ was buried,

that Christ was raised,

and that Christ appeared.

The gospel is the story of the crucial events in the life of Jesus Christ. Instead of "four spiritual laws," which for many holds up our salvation culture, the earliest gospel concerned four "events" or "chapters" in the life of Jesus Christ.

We perhaps need to remind ourselves of something at the grassroots level: the word *gospel* was used in the world of Jews at the time of the apostles to *announce* something, to *declare* something as good news—the word *euangelion* always means good news. "To gospel" is to herald, to proclaim, and to declare something about something. To put this together: the gospel is to announce good news about key events in the life of Jesus Christ. To gospel for Paul was to tell, announce, declare, and shout aloud the Story of Jesus Christ as the saving news of God.

. . . The important words used are "according to the Scriptures." The apostolic gospel is an "according-to-Scriptures telling of the Story of Jesus."

. . . The Story of Jesus Christ is locked into one people, one history, and one Scripture: it makes sense only as it follows and completes the Story of Israel. (Pages 49–50, KJG)

There is a Person at the very core of the gospel of Paul, and until that Person is put into the center of centers in Paul's gospel, we will not comprehend his—scratch that—the apostles' gospel accurately. The gospel Story of Jesus Christ *is a story about Jesus as Messiah, Jesus as Lord, Jesus as Savior, and Jesus as Son.* It is sometimes forgotten that "Christ" is the Greek translation of the Hebrew word *Messiah*. The word *Messiah* means "anointed King" and "Lord" and "Ruler." Lord means, well, "Lord," and the word *Son* here certainly means the anointed king of Israel, as in Psalm 2. So, the emphasis here in the gospel is that Jesus is Lord over all.

But he is king as a result of battle. The Story of Jesus, according to paragraph C, involves Jesus' triumphal victory over "all dominion, authority and power." This victory goes even deeper and broader: Jesus, Messiah and Lord and Son, will conquer "death" as well. Any reading of 1 Corinthians 15, then, will immediately fasten our ideas on Jesus as the center of the Story. (Page 55, KJG)

We are tempted to turn the story of what God is doing in this world through Israel and Jesus Christ into a story about *me and my own personal salvation*. In other words, the plan [of salvation] has a way of cutting the story from a story about God and God's Messiah and people into a story about God and one person—me—and this story shifts from Christ and community to individualism. We need the latter without cutting off the former.

. . . a gospel culture is one shaped by the Story of Israel and the Story of Jesus Christ, a story that moves from creation to consummation, a story that tells the whole Story of Jesus and not just a Good Friday story, and a story that tells not just of personal salvation but of God being "all in all." It tells the story that Jesus, not any human ruler, is the Lord over all. (Page 62, KJG)

Reflection questions on the reading

1. What do you think about the idea of an oral tradition of the gospel being passed through the apostles before the Gospels were written down? The Gospels appear in our Bibles before Paul's letters, but the letters were probably written first. Is this something you had heard before, or was this a new idea to you?

2. What does the reading say "to gospel" meant for Paul?

3. How does it change your perspective on the gospel to center the story on Jesus instead of centering it on your personal salvation?

PRAYER

Think about the story of Jesus as being an announcement of very good news. Thank God in your prayers today for the good news that Paul and the other apostles passed down to us. Thank God for the Scriptures, both Old Testament and New Testament, that record this story and this good news.

As you conclude your prayer time, pray the Lord's Prayer:

> *Our Father in heaven, hallowed be your name, your kingdom come, your will be done, on earth as it is in heaven. Give us today our daily bread. And forgive us our debts, as we also have forgiven our debtors. And lead us not into temptation, but deliver us from the evil one, for yours is the kingdom and the power and the glory forever. Amen. (Matthew 6:9–13)*

ACTION

Search on the internet for images of Herod the Great, Herod Antipas, and Tiberius Caesar, rulers in Jesus' time. Then search for images of Jesus. How do their appearances differ (clothing, poses, hair, crowns, jewelry) in the artistic depictions? How do various presentations of Jesus as King contrast with the presentations of earthly kings and rulers?

REFLECTION

What do you think about kings? What thoughts or images come to mind? How would you describe a king? How does the idea of Jesus as King affect you? Do you see that as a positive or a negative concept? How does Jesus reshape your ideas of kingship? Journal your thoughts.

▪ GROUP DISCUSSION ▪

When your group meeting begins, say the Jesus Creed together:

Hear, O Israel, the Lord our God, the Lord is one. Love the Lord your God with all your heart, with all your soul, with all your mind, and with all your strength. The second is this: love your neighbor as yourself. There is no commandment greater than these.

The following questions are based on the personal study you already have completed. Monitor how much time your group has for discussion and answer as many of these questions together as you can.

READING AND BIBLE STUDY

▪ What is the gospel you have received so far in your life?

▪ What have you passed on to others?

▪ If you were the Christians in Corinth receiving Paul's letter, and this was the only gospel you had ever heard, what impact would that have on your view of Jesus?

▪ When asked to quote one Bible verse that explains "the gospel," many Christians reference John 3:16. If someone in your group can recite it, have them do so. Otherwise, look it up in a Bible and read it out loud. What view of gospel and salvation does John 3:16 give?

▪ What view of gospel and salvation does 1 Corinthians 15 give?

▪ How do these verses from John and 1 Corinthians differ?

PRAYER

A common view of prayer is that it mostly consists of asking God for things. How did it change your view of prayer to spend your prayer time *thanking* God this week?

ACTION

Has anyone in your group visited or lived in a country with a monarchy? How did that affect their view of kingship?

Search for a video of a ceremony welcoming a new king, such as the inauguration of King Willem-Alexander of the Netherlands in 2013, the swearing in of King Felipe VI of Spain in 2014, or the coronation of King Tupou VI of Tonga in 2015. Watch part of it together as a group.

Now have someone in the group look up and read Revelation 19:11–16 out loud. This is from John's vision of the future of God's kingdom. How does the ceremony of an earthly king compare or contrast with the image of the reign of King Jesus?

REFLECTION

As you journaled this week, what did you discover about how your existing thoughts on kings influence your view of Jesus as king?

GROUP PRAYER

Each group member can share something they are thankful for this week, and one group member can pray to conclude, echoing the thanks of the group to God.

As your group meeting ends, pray the Lord's Prayer together:

> *Our Father in heaven, hallowed be your name, your kingdom come, your will be done, on earth as it is in heaven. Give us today our daily bread. And forgive us our debts, as we also have forgiven our debtors. And lead us not into temptation, but deliver us from the evil one, for yours is the kingdom and the power and the glory forever. Amen. (Matthew 6:9–13)*

REST

Do you enjoy relaxing by watching movies? Entertaining stories can sometimes teach us better than direct instruction because they can lower our defenses and make us more receptive to understanding, or they can help us view things in new ways. As you rest from your study, watch a movie about a king and see what new ideas about Jesus' kingship come from the experience.

3

LESSON 3

THE GOSPEL OF JESUS

Learning intent: Disciples will learn that Jesus preached the gospel by preaching himself as the good news.

Spiritual formation intent: Disciples will focus their idea of the gospel not around their own sin and forgiveness but around the much bigger picture of Jesus himself as the good news.

■ PERSONAL STUDY ■

READING

As you begin your discipleship time today, say the Jesus Creed out loud:

Hear, O Israel, the Lord our God, the Lord is one. Love the Lord your God with all your heart, with all your soul, with all your mind, and with all your strength. The second is this: love your neighbor as yourself. There is no commandment greater than these.

The question we are asking is this: Did Jesus preach the gospel? But that does not mean, Did Jesus preach personal salvation or preach justification by faith (no matter how true and important those concepts are). Instead, we have to move to a different plane. If the gospel is the saving Story of Jesus that completes the Story of Israel, the question is actually more refined: *Did Jesus preach that he was the completion of Israel's Story?*

If he did, Jesus preached the apostolic gospel, whether he preached the Plan of Salvation or not. So the gospel question is . . . *"Did Jesus preach himself as the completion of Israel's Story in such a way that he was the saving story himself?"* . . .

This new question shifts the entire focus from *the benefits of salvation that we experience* to the *Person who himself is the good news.* (Page 108, KJG)

First—and perhaps this is the easiest to miss as well as the least interesting because we have heard it before—*Jesus believed the kingdom of God was breaking into history.* Two texts in the Gospels make this abundantly clear. The summary passage of Jesus' preaching according to Mark is: "The time has come. . . . The kingdom of God *has come near*" (Mark 1:15). . . . The second text evokes something even closer, so close one has to say, "It is here!" In Matthew 12:28 Jesus says, "But if it is by the Spirit of God that I drive out demons, then the kingdom of God *has come upon you.*" (Page 112, KJG)

Second, Jesus declares a *new society in the land.* The long-awaited kingdom society will be marked by radical changes, and to express this vision for what God is about to do, Jesus clips lines from Isaiah's Servant song opening up Isaiah 61 and applies those words to himself in Luke 4:18–19. . . . Clearly, words shaped for the exiles of Isaiah's day and embodied in the "Servant" are taken up by Jesus to apply to himself and for those whom he sees in "exile": the poor, the imprisoned, blind, and the oppressed. All of this is empowered by the Spirit.

Third, Jesus declares *a new citizenship.* . . . What Jesus said in his famous sermon shocks and startles because all the "wrong" people are "in" and all the "right" people are "out." What we see here is a radical reversal of the citizens of the kingdom. Luke 6:20–26 reads clearly and needs no commentary. (Pages 112–13, KJG)

Fourth, the wording of the Gospels throws immediate clarity that the kingdom Jesus is announcing is the kingdom *of God.* This kingdom contrasts with that of the Jewish ruler Herod Antipas and the Roman ruler Tiberius. Here we have a radical call by Jesus: he is calling everyone to submit to *God, the God of Israel, YHWH, the Creator and Covenant maker.* The Lord's Prayer of Jesus, which expresses the heart of his vision and mission, begins on this very theme:

> Our Father in heaven,
> hallowed be your name,
> your kingdom come,
> your will be done,
> on earth as it is in heaven. (Matthew 6:9–10) . . .

Fifth, and now we come to the center of what gospeling is all about, and for some weird reason scholars and preachers alike skip right over the point, Jesus declares *he is at the center of the kingdom of God.* . . . Luke 7:22–23. (Page 114, KJG)

. . . Jesus not only believed the kingdom was connected to him and to his mission and teachings, *but he believed the kingdom of God was now breaking into history in himself.* (Page 116, KJG)

Who did Jesus think Jesus was? We could take the Luke 7 passage we cited above and say Jesus is the kingdom-bringer and Isaiah-role-completer, or we could put our spoon into the confession of Peter and see Jesus as Messiah, or we could test the waters of different passages, some of which are barely even noticed by Bible readers today. . . . Jesus was totally into *preaching himself as the center of God's plan for Israel.* . . .

Did Jesus preach the gospel? Yes, he preached the gospel because the gospel is the saving Story of Jesus completing Israel's Story, and Jesus clearly set himself at the center of God's saving plan for Israel. . . . The Gospels, by their very nature, tell a Story of Jesus on center stage on every page. The Gospels are the gospel and Jesus preached the gospel. . . . Jesus preached Jesus and Paul preached Jesus and Peter preached Jesus. Preaching Jesus is preaching the gospel. . . . To respond to Jesus was to respond to the gospel; to respond to the gospel was to respond to Jesus. (Pages 127–28, KJG)

Reflection questions on the reading

1. What does the reading say are five things Jesus believed and declared?

   First: _____

   Second: _____

   Third: _____

   Fourth: _____

   Fifth: _____

2. What did Jesus think about himself? Who did he think he was?

3. Did Jesus preach the gospel? How and why?

BIBLE STUDY

Expectations for God's Work through Jesus (Psalm 72; Luke 1 and 7)

In the reading, we looked at what Jesus thought and said about himself. In the Bible study, we will consider what other people thought and said about Jesus. This is more reading than the previous Bible study sections, so allow yourself plenty of time. It all ties together at the end.

Read Psalm 72:1–7.

1. As the Jews of Jesus' time heard this psalm read, this poetic prayer for the king, how do you think it shaped their expectations of the coming messianic king?

Read Luke 1:46–55.

Mary, pregnant with Jesus, is visiting her relative Elizabeth, who is pregnant with John the Baptist. Luke records this song that Mary sings about what she believes God is doing through her baby.

1. What emotions characterize Mary's words?

2. Mary was likely poor and also ostracized due to her pregnancy outside of marriage. How do you think her personal circumstances affected which hopes she focused on in God's work?

Read Luke 1:67–79.

Zechariah is the husband of Elizabeth and the father of John the Baptist. After the birth of John, the cousin of Jesus, Zechariah prophesies in song about Jesus and John.

1. Zechariah was a priest. How do you think his vocation shaped the hopes he focused on in God's work?

2. What does Zechariah think God is doing through Jesus? What does he think God will do through John?

Read Luke 7:18–23.

Now John and Jesus are grown up and both working in their ministries. Here you can read the exchange between some of John's disciples and Jesus.

1. Compare Jesus' words to John's disciples here with Jesus' words announcing his ministry to the people of Nazareth in Luke 4. What connections do you see between the two passages?

2. Now look through all the passages from this week's study again and make a list of the repeated words and themes.

PRAYER

Write a poetic prayer in the style of Psalm 72 or Mary's song or Zechariah's song. What are the specific hopes you have for God to act in your life, in your culture, in your time? How can you praise God for what God has already done, is doing, and will do? If you are musical, try setting it to music.

As you conclude your prayer time, pray the Lord's Prayer:

> *Our Father in heaven, hallowed be your name, your kingdom come, your will be done, on earth as it is in heaven. Give us today our daily bread. And forgive us our debts, as we also have forgiven our debtors. And lead us not into temptation, but deliver us from the evil one, for yours is the kingdom and the power and the glory forever. Amen. (Matthew 6:9–13)*

ACTION

Find and listen to a musical recording of Mary's song, the Magnificat, online (there are many!).

REFLECTION

- How do you imagine John the Baptist responded to the report his disciples brought back from Jesus? Try writing a description of the scene and some dialogue. If John had grown up hearing his father repeat his song, and his mother repeat Mary's song, what expectations would that have created in John for what the Messiah would do? Do you think Jesus fulfilled or disappointed John's expectations?

▪ GROUP DISCUSSION ▪

When your group meeting begins, say the Jesus Creed together:

Hear, O Israel, the Lord our God, the Lord is one. Love the Lord your God with all your heart, with all your soul, with all your mind, and with all your strength. The second is this: love your neighbor as yourself. There is no commandment greater than these.

The following questions are based on the personal study you already have completed. Monitor how much time your group has for discussion and answer as many of these questions together as you can.

READING

▪ If you had been asked the question, "Did Jesus preach the gospel?" before you had read this lesson, what would you have said?

▪ Now how would you explain to someone that Jesus preached the gospel?

▪ What do you think Jesus knew about his mission and ministry at various stages in his life?

BIBLE STUDY

▪ Based on expectations from the Hebrew Scriptures (what Christians call the Old Testament), what did Mary and Zechariah expect God to do in Jesus?

▪ What themes did you notice in common between the songs of Mary and Zechariah?

▪ How did Jesus live out God's work among the people through his ministry?

■ Do you think Jesus lived up to his mother's expectations?

PRAYER

If you are willing, share your psalm or poetic prayer with the group. Also, what did you think of the experience of writing it?

ACTION

Have one of your group members dramatically perform Mary's song or Zechariah's song. How does hearing it read with emotion affect your understanding of the text?

REFLECTION

Did anyone in your group really get into writing the scene with John and his disciples? If so, try acting it out with your group members.

GROUP PRAYER

Let everyone in the group share about something in their lives that needs God's intervention. Ask one person to write down all the needs and pray for them out loud.

As your group meeting ends, pray the Lord's Prayer together:

Our Father in heaven, hallowed be your name, your kingdom come, your will be done, on earth as it is in heaven. Give us today our daily bread. And forgive us our debts, as we also have forgiven our debtors. And lead us not into temptation, but deliver us from the evil one, for yours is the kingdom and the power and the glory forever. Amen. (Matthew 6:9–13)

REST

Have your expectations of God ever been disappointed? Give yourself permission and the emotional time and space to experience those thoughts and feelings, even if they seem negative or uncomfortable. Try being honest with God about this. See if you can figure out how to experience rest in God in the midst of this uncertainty or lack of fulfillment.

4

LESSON 4

THE GOSPEL OF PETER

Learning intent: Disciples will learn more about the apostolic gospel message by examining Peter's gospeling sermons and claims about Jesus.

Spiritual formation intent: Disciples will practice putting into words their own gospel messages that echo the apostolic gospel.

■ PERSONAL STUDY ■

READING

As you begin your discipleship time today, say the Jesus Creed out loud:

Hear, O Israel, the Lord our God, the Lord is one. Love the Lord your God with all your heart, with all your soul, with all your mind, and with all your strength. The second is this: love your neighbor as yourself. There is no commandment greater than these.

From Peter's world-transforming sermon in Acts 2 to Paul's sermon on the Areopagus in Acts 17, it was the Story of Israel that shaped how they gospeled. If we want to get "gospel" right, we will need to remember that in the heart of that apostolic gospel tradition in 1 Corinthians 15 is "according to the Scriptures." . . . the sermons in the book of Acts put muscle *and fat* on that very "according to the Scriptures" bone in the apostolic gospel tradition.

What, then, did "according to the Scriptures" look like when they preached? In Peter's first gospel sermon, as sketched in Acts 2:13–21, he quotes Joel 2:28–32 and Psalm 16:8–11 and 110:1. . . . Peter journeys backward in time into the depths of Israel's Story so he can show that the whole story points forward to Jesus Christ and Pentecost. Peter's depth of insight and the dexterity of his memory in Acts 2 reveal what might be the single most significant theological shift among the apostles: Jesus' resurrection and the profound experience with the Holy Spirit at Pentecost led the apostles into a "hermeneutical revolution." They suddenly had new eyes to reread and reinterpret the Old Testament from the perspective of the Story of Jesus. We need to remind ourselves constantly that the apostles, who all gospeled like this, didn't have iPads, iPods, or iPhones with a Bible search engine that could chase down a favorite word in the Bible. The apostles had memory, and that memory was reconfigured by the Story of Jesus so much that their way of reading the Bible was transformed.

In his second gospel sermon, found in Acts 3:22–23, Peter quotes Deuteronomy 18:15, 18–19, that famous passage in the Old Testament about the future prophet-like-Moses. Jesus is that prophet according to Peter's gospel. At Acts 3:25 Peter quotes Genesis 22:18 or 26:4—both mentioning the blessing of gentiles—to establish the Abrahamic origins of the gospel. In Acts 10:43 Peter finishes off the gospeling event at Cornelius's house by making a claim that only folks as far removed as we are can miss its extravagance: "All the prophets testify about" Jesus Christ. . . .

These citations of Scripture aren't apologetic props in a sermon that could get by without those props. No, the apostles' gospel was the Story of Jesus resolving the Story of Israel. The texts the apostles quoted from the Old Testament weren't props; they were the light posts to help Israel find its way from Abraham to Jesus. (Pages 133–34, KJG)

What the prophets were yearning for in images that they themselves ached to comprehend and what they were glimpsing in all but fully comprehensible ways suddenly appeared one day in the land of Israel, and his name wasYeshua ben Yoseph and Miriam. Once they encountered him, their Bible became a new book *precisely because they read it as gospel*.

Back to Peter's gospeling.

Peter's gospeling also puts the life of a live body on the bones of 1 Corinthians 15, and that means his gospel involved telling the full Story of Jesus Christ, including his life, his death, his resurrection, his exaltation, the gift of the Holy Spirit, his second coming, and the wrapping up of history so that God would be all in all. The reason we have to say this is because too often we have:

reduced the life of Jesus to Good Friday, and therefore
reduced the gospel to the crucifixion, and then soterians have
reduced Jesus to transactions of a Savior.

Not so in the early gospeling, for in those early apostolic sermons, we see the whole life of Jesus. In fact, if they gave an emphasis to one dimension of the life of Jesus, it was the resurrection. The apostolic gospel could not have been signified or painted or sketched with a crucifix. That gospel wanted expression as an empty cross because of the empty tomb. (Pages 135–36, KJG)

Peter made stupendous claims about Jesus; either they are true or they are ridiculous because they are that stupendous. Peter's Jesus of Nazareth, the one who lived and died and who was raised and ascended and enthroned, is both *Messiah of Israel and Lord of the whole world*. Those are the terms of the early gospeling in the book of Acts, and if we want to be faithful to the Bible, those should be our terms as well. Those titles for Jesus tell the gospel Story of Jesus. (Page 138, KJG)

Peter reads a Bible that leads him to see God at work guiding the Story of Israel into the Story of Jesus, and the Jesus of that story is Israel's true King and the Lord over all . . . Peter knows this because God raised Jesus from the grave. There are other terms Peter uses for Jesus, including "servant" (3:13), "the Holy and Righteous One" (3:14), "the author of life" (3:15), and the "prophet" (3:22–23), but these supplement his two major terms, "Messiah" and "Lord." All the apostles saw Jesus as Messiah and Lord, and all you have to do is open your Bible to any of the New Testament letters and these terms jump off the page. For the apostles, it was all about King Jesus. (Page 139, KJG)

Reflection questions on the reading

1. How did Peter use his memory of the Hebrew Scriptures in preaching his gospel sermons?

2. Why can't we reduce the apostolic gospel to the crucifixion?

3. What are some of the terms Peter uses for Jesus?

BIBLE STUDY

The clearest example of Peter's whole-life-of-Jesus with an emphasis on cross-leading-to-resurrection gospel is seen at Acts 10:36–42, and I would urge you to read this entirely and slowly. . . .

This text is not quite complete, but if one adds together what we find in Acts 2:22–35; 3:13–15, 19–21; and 10:37–42, we discover that Peter preached the whole Story of Jesus as Messiah. (Page 136, KJG)

Peter's Gospel (Acts 3 and Acts 10)

Peter and John, two of Jesus' closest disciples, were going to the temple in Jerusalem to pray one afternoon. They saw a lame beggar, and when Peter used the authority of Jesus' name, God healed the man. Many Jewish people gathered around, and Peter preached this gospel sermon to them.

Read Acts 3:12–26.

1. What references does Peter make to the Story of Israel?

2. What parts of Jesus' story does Peter tell?

Peter was summoned to Caesarea to the home of Cornelius, a powerful gentile centurion who respected God and wanted to hear Peter's message. Peter preached this gospel sermon to the large group of Cornelius's gentile family and friends who filled his home.

Read Acts 10:34–43.

1. What references does Peter make to the Story of Israel?

2. What parts of Jesus' story does Peter tell?

3. How does Peter tell the gospel differently to Jews in Acts 3 and to gentiles in Acts 10?

4. Sum up Peter's gospel in two or three sentences or in a bulleted list.

PRAYER

Cornelius "prayed to God regularly" (Acts 10:2) even before he became a follower of Jesus. One day, God responded to Cornelius's prayer by giving him a vision of an angel who brought a message about Peter, leading Cornelius to invite Peter to visit. Have you ever experienced an answer or response to prayer? It doesn't have to be as dramatic as an angelic vision!

Pray today about something that troubles you, that you would really like to hear from God about. Be patient as you sit and wait for God to respond. Be open to the many different ways God might communicate with you.

As you conclude your prayer time, pray the Lord's Prayer:

> *Our Father in heaven, hallowed be your name, your kingdom come, your will be done, on earth as it is in heaven. Give us today our daily bread. And forgive us our debts, as we also have forgiven our debtors. And lead us not into temptation, but deliver us from the evil one, for yours is the kingdom and the power and the glory forever. Amen. (Matthew 6:9–13)*

ACTION

The reading in this lesson pointed out that the apostles' memory of Scripture helped them preach the gospel to various audiences. Choose a verse or two from one of Peter's or Paul's gospel sermons and work on memorizing it so that you can include it in your gospeling.

REFLECTION

Think of two of your friends with very different religious or non-religious backgrounds. If they asked you to tell them about Jesus, how would you give them a gospel message that was contextualized for their understanding, just like Peter did for those to whom he ministered?

▨ Write your two different gospel messages in the space below. Try to include your memorized verse from this lesson's action point in both messages.

■ GROUP DISCUSSION ■

When your group meeting begins, say the Jesus Creed together:

Hear, O Israel, the Lord our God, the Lord is one. Love the Lord your God with all your heart, with all your soul, with all your mind, and with all your strength. The second is this: love your neighbor as yourself. There is no commandment greater than these.

The following questions are based on the personal study you already have completed. Monitor how much time your group has for discussion and answer as many of these questions together as you can.

READING

■ Have you read much in the Gospels about Peter or heard sermons about him? What do you remember about him? If you need a refresher, here are some stories about Peter:

- Peter disagrees with Jesus (Matthew 16:22–23)
- Peter falls asleep praying (Matthew 26:40)
- Peter attacks someone with a sword (John 18:10)
- Peter denies Jesus publicly (John 18:15–27)

■ How is the behavior of Peter in the book of Acts different from his words and actions in the Gospels?

■ What do you think made the change in him?

BIBLE STUDY

▪ What was the same and what was different between Peter's two sermons in the Bible study?

▪ Look up the passages again (Acts 3 and Acts 10) as a group and read the verses that follow the sermons. What were the responses from the two groups to the sermons?

PRAYER

As you prayed this week, did you experience any responses from God? Can you share about another time when God has answered a prayer?

ACTION

Peter and John were on their way to a regularly scheduled time of group prayer in the temple. Have you ever been to a gathering of other Christians just to pray together? Has this been part of your normal schedule at some point in your life? Share about your experiences with prayer meetings.

Do you know of any area churches that host prayer meetings? Plan to attend one together as a group—put it on your calendars during your group meeting now.

REFLECTION

Share how your different gospel messages changed based on your imagined audiences.

What could you do to create an opportunity to actually share those messages with the people you imagined talking to?

GROUP PRAYER

Peter called on God's power for a man's physical healing, and God did a miracle to heal the man. Does anyone in your group need physical healing today? Pray for that person together, and if they feel comfortable with it, lay your hands on them.

Share the healing needs of other people you know. If group members are willing, let them pray out loud for their friend or loved one in need of healing.

If you hear any follow-up reports that God intervened and brought healing, share that with the group in the future.

As your group meeting ends, pray the Lord's Prayer together:

Our Father in heaven, hallowed be your name, your kingdom come, your will be done, on earth as it is in heaven. Give us today our daily bread. And forgive us our debts, as we also have forgiven our debtors. And lead us not into temptation, but deliver us from the evil one, for yours is the kingdom and the power and the glory forever. Amen. (Matthew 6:9–13)

REST

Part of God's process in bringing the gospel to Cornelius and his household was speaking to Peter in a resting vision (Acts 10:9–17). Peter quoted the prophet Joel saying that God would speak in dreams and visions (Acts 2:17–18). Consider that God could speak to you in a dream. As you rest from your studies, tell God that you are open to hearing through a dream or vision, and see what God brings to your attention.

5

LESSON 5

WHAT IS GOSPELING TODAY?

Learning intent: Disciples will learn how to gospel like the apostles, centering their gospel message on the Story of Jesus.

Spiritual formation intent: Disciples will begin learning to look to the example of Jesus to help them shape their life choices and priorities.

▪ PERSONAL STUDY ▪

READING

As you begin your discipleship time today, say the Jesus Creed out loud:

Hear, O Israel, the Lord our God, the Lord is one. Love the Lord your God with all your heart, with all your soul, with all your mind, and with all your strength. The second is this: love your neighbor as yourself. There is no commandment greater than these.

The task of evangelism, what I am calling "gospeling," is no less demanding and difficult today than it was in the time of Peter and Paul. It is also in no less need of creative adaptations to one's audience. Perhaps we need more of the boldness that came upon the apostles through a fresh blowing of the Spirit. Perhaps we need to pray as those early Christians prayed: "After they prayed, the place where they were meeting was shaken. And they were all filled with the Holy Spirit and spoke the word of God boldly" (Acts 4:31).

Or perhaps it is the almost complete absence of resurrection theology in much of gospeling today that explains our lack of boldness. At any rate, we need to recover more of that early, emboldened Christian resurrection gospel.

If we put this gospel now into one bundle, and if we focus on how that gospel was preached by the apostles, the book of Acts reveals that the gospel is, first of all, *framed by Israel's Story*, the narration of the saving Story of Jesus—his life, his death, his resurrection, his exaltation, and his coming again—as the completion of the Story of Israel.

Second, the gospel centers on the lordship of *Jesus*. In ways that anticipate the Nicene Creed, the gospel of Peter and Paul is anchored in an exalted view of Jesus. Jesus is seen as suffering, saving, ruling, and judging because he is the Messiah and the Lord and the Davidic Savior. He is now exalted at the right hand of God.

Third, gospeling involves *summoning people to respond*. Apostolic gospeling is incomplete until it lovingly but firmly summons those who hear the gospel to repentance, to faith in Jesus Christ, and to baptism.

Fourth, the gospel *saves and redeems*. The apostolic gospel promises forgiveness, the gift of God's Holy Spirit, and justification.

I rest my case now: these four points sketch the gospel wherever we look in the New Testament. This gospel is found in Paul's own words in 1 Corinthians 15; it is the gospel of the Gospels, it is the gospel of Jesus himself, it is the gospel of Peter, and it is the gospel of Paul—according to Luke's own sketch of Paul's sermons. There is one and only one gospel, and it was passed on from Jesus to the apostles to their churches. It is this gospel, and this gospel alone, that glues the New Testament into unity. If we want to be New Testament Christians, this gospel must once again become our gospel. (Pages 148–49, KJG)

We are not creating a false alternative here. The latter can be done within the former, but much of the soterian approach to evangelism today fastens on Jesus as (personal) Savior and dodges Jesus as Messiah and Lord. If there is any pervasive heresy today, it's right here. Anyone who can preach the gospel and not make Jesus' exalted lordship the focal point simply isn't preaching the apostolic gospel. . . . (Pages 149–50, KJG)

First, our gospeling tends to reduce and aim at one and only one target: the sinner's heart. Evangelism's focus is on the individual person, and it is on getting that person to admit that he or she is a sinner, and then getting them to receive Jesus Christ as Savior and a solution to the sin problem. . . . the apostolic gospel can't be reduced to a gospel of sin management because it was a gospel of Jesus-declaration (that included the defeat of sin and death).

Don't get me wrong, the apostolic gospel did promise the forgiveness of sins. But it did so by telling a (saving) story about Jesus. (Page 160, KJG)

Second, the question that many are asking today reveals that there's not enough Jesus in our gospel. The question is this: Did Jesus preach the gospel? If we are tempted for even a passing moment to wonder if the Gospels preach the gospel, then we have fallen from the apostolic gospel. Why? It was the apostolic generation that called Mark (and probably Matthew) the "gospel." Why? Because the gospel is the completion of Israel's Story in the Story of Jesus, and that is precisely what the Gospels do. . . .

We need to talk more about Jesus and know that telling others about Jesus is half the battle when it comes to fear of evangelism. We can improve our evangelism simply by learning to approach the gospel in the apostolic manner. (Page 161, KJG)

Reflection questions on the reading

1. What is "gospeling"?

2. What changes in your perspective when you think in terms of gospeling instead of evangelism?

3. What is the difference between apostolic gospeling and Plan of Salvation gospeling?

4. List several ways you could get more Jesus into your gospel:

BIBLE STUDY

The Story of Jesus (Mark 1–8)

Prepare for a lot of Bible reading in this lesson! We need to talk more about Jesus as we gospel, and one of the best ways to get inspired to talk more about Jesus is to learn more from him. As we follow King Jesus, reading the four Gospels that tell his story is an ongoing practice we should develop. Start this week by reading the first half of the Gospel of Mark. It's the shortest of the four, and it's full of action, so you can get through it (relatively) fast. Depending on your reading speed, you can probably read the whole book in under an hour. Scot gives students in his Jesus and the Gospels course the assignment to read all four Gospels during the semester, each in one sitting. Set aside at least half an hour and read the first eight chapters of Mark. Try to read them in one sitting so you get caught up in the story. Or you can listen to an audio Bible—try the free app YouVersion.

Read Mark 1–8.

1. Describe your overall impression as you finished reading these chapters. What do you think of Jesus right now?

2. Skim back through the chapters again and write down the key teachings of Jesus in these chapters.

3. At the end of chapter 8, Jesus speaks honestly about the cost of being his disciple. What is your response to these hard words?

4. What did you think of the experience of reading a large section of Scripture at one time? Is this a practice you would like to incorporate more into your development as a disciple of Jesus in the future?

PRAYER

The first chapter of Mark records that Jesus got up before the morning light and went outdoors to pray (Mark 1:35). Plan a time this week to wake up early and go somewhere outside to pray. If you work late shifts or aren't able to get outdoors, try praying at a different time than normal, and see if you can find a space for solitude.

When you pray, think about the role of faith in prayer. Jesus chastised some of his disciples for their lack of faith when they asked him to calm the storm (Mark 4:40), and he praised a woman who came to him for healing because of her faith (Mark 5:34). Why is faith important? Do you have faith when you pray?

As you conclude your prayer time, pray the Lord's Prayer:

Our Father in heaven, hallowed be your name, your kingdom come, your will be done, on earth as it is in heaven. Give us today our daily bread. And forgive us our debts, as we also have forgiven our debtors. And lead us not into temptation, but deliver us from the evil one, for yours is the kingdom and the power and the glory forever. Amen. (Matthew 6:9–13)

ACTION

Search on Spotify or YouTube for the Rend Collective songs "Build Your Kingdom Here" and "Hymn of the Ages." Listen to the songs or watch the music videos. The tone or style of these songs could be described as "anthem." How do the songs affect your heart and your thoughts about the church as the kingdom of God and Jesus as king? What do they inspire you to want to do?

REFLECTION

Mark records some of Jesus' parables in chapter 4. Parables are extended metaphors or similes that teach a lesson.

Think of an analogy for the kingdom of God or the gospel. Write a parable teaching your creative lesson.

▪ GROUP DISCUSSION ▪

When your group meeting begins, say the Jesus Creed together:

Hear, O Israel, the Lord our God, the Lord is one. Love the Lord your God with all your heart, with all your soul, with all your mind, and with all your strength. The second is this: love your neighbor as yourself. There is no commandment greater than these.

The following questions are based on the personal study you already have completed. Monitor how much time your group has for discussion and answer as many of these questions together as you can.

READING

How have these lessons shaped or reshaped your understanding of the gospel?

What are you reorienting in your thinking and actions to move toward a more apostolic, Jesus-centered gospel?

BIBLE STUDY

What impressions of Jesus did you gather from the study?

How did you find the experience of reading half a gospel at one time?

What account of healing in these chapters stood out to you the most, and why?

ACTION

The public reading of Scripture was a regular and important practice for the church in the first few centuries. They read the Gospels in their house church gatherings as well as the Hebrew Scriptures and letters from the apostles. Ask someone in the group to stand and read Mark 9 out loud to the group—dramatically!—the whole chapter, as if you were all part of an early gathering of Christians.

Optional activity: If someone from the group would like to take this on, plan a meal of bread and fish for the group. Consider serving it in baskets and have a picnic on the ground. Break the bread and give thanks to God for it. How does using your senses like this help you imagine life for the early disciples? What do you think it was like for them to see Jesus provide food for thousands of people and for them all to eat this miraculous meal together?

PRAYER

This particular group guide places the prayer discussion after the Action so that you can bring Mark 9:23–24 into your discussion on faith. Ask someone in the group to read those verses now. Notice the prayer of the father.

- In your personal study, what conclusions did you draw about the role of faith in prayer? How could the father's prayer in Mark 9:24 help you when you feel like you don't have enough faith to pray?

- What was it like to pray outside? Where did you go?

REFLECTION

Share your parable ideas with each other. What did you choose for your analogy? Either summarize and explain it or read what you wrote.

GROUP PRAYER

Each person can share a need or concern for prayer. After each person shares, someone else in the group can volunteer to pray for them, and then the group can pause for that prayer right then. Continue until each person has had a chance to share a request.

As your group meeting ends, pray the Lord's Prayer together:

Our Father in heaven, hallowed be your name, your kingdom come, your will be done, on earth as it is in heaven. Give us today our daily bread. And forgive us our debts, as we also have forgiven our debtors. And lead us not into temptation, but deliver us from the evil one, for yours is the kingdom and the power and the glory forever. Amen. (Matthew 6:9–13)

REST

Jesus, as a faithful Jew, generally followed the Sabbath practice of his culture, setting aside Saturday for worship and for rest from work. He challenged people's interpretations and observations of the practice, and he broke the barriers of accepted Sabbath practice in his works and his teachings, but for the most part he participated in the religion of his people. For example, in Mark 6:2, Jesus went to the synagogue to teach as part of his Sabbath observance. Mark also records some of Jesus' reinterpretations of the Sabbath. In Mark 2:23–28, he explained that Sabbath was made for people—it was a gift to them, not a burden. In Mark 3:1–6, he healed on the Sabbath and pointed out that healing was doing good.

As you develop your personal convictions and practices of rest and worship in your life, how can you use Jesus' example of faithfulness and flexibility to decide how to honor God through worship and rest? What could a personal Sabbath practice look like for you?

6

LESSON 6

HOW DO WE CREATE A GOSPEL CULTURE?

Learning intent: Disciples will learn to read the Bible as God's words to God's people.
Spiritual formation intent: Disciples will ask themselves, "What is my relationship to the Bible?" and, more importantly, "What is my relationship to the God of the Bible?"

■ PERSONAL STUDY ■

READING

As you begin your discipleship time today, say the Jesus Creed out loud:

Hear, O Israel, the Lord our God, the Lord is one. Love the Lord your God with all your heart, with all your soul, with all your mind, and with all your strength. The second is this: love your neighbor as yourself. There is no commandment greater than these.

How Do We Create a Gospel Culture?

First, *we have to become People of the Story.* One of the most common responses I've had to lecturing about the gospel occurs when someone approaches me to say something like this: "Scot, thanks for your lecture. During that lecture I committed myself to reading the Bible from front to back for the first time." To become a gospel culture we've got to begin with becoming people of the Book, but not just as a Book, but as the story that shapes us. . . .

Second, *we need to immerse ourselves even more into the Story of Jesus.* The gospel is that the Story of Israel comes to its definitive completeness in the Story of Jesus, and this means we have to become People of the Story-that-is-complete-in-Jesus. There is one and only one way to become People of the Story of Jesus: we need to soak ourselves in the Story of Jesus by reading, pondering, digesting, and mulling over in our heads and hearts the Four Gospels. Genuine soaking in this story always leads to the Story of Israel because it is only in that story that the Story of Jesus makes sense. (Page 169, KJG)

I see another way for us to become people of the Story of Jesus. . . . The church calendar is all about the Story of Jesus, and I know of nothing—other than regular soaking in the Bible—that can "gospelize" our life more than the church calendar. It begins with Advent, then Christmas, then Epiphany, then After Epiphany, then Lent, then the Great Triduum (Maundy Thursday, Good Friday, and the Paschal Vigil on Saturday evening), Easter, and then After Pentecost—with Ordinary Time shaping the calendar until Advent. Ordinary Time is the time to focus on the life and teachings of Jesus. Anyone who is half aware of the calendar in a church that is consciously devoted to focusing on these events in their theological and biblical contexts will be exposed every year to the whole gospel, to the whole Story of Israel coming to its saving completion in the Story of Jesus. (Pages 170–71, KJG)

Third, *we need to see how the apostles' writings take the Story of Israel and the Story of Jesus into the next generation and into a different culture, and how this generation led all the way to our generation.* . . . Jesus clearly told his disciples, and I think here of John 14–17; Matthew 28:16–20; and Acts 1:8, that *his story was to continue in the story of the church.*

We have a responsibility to Jesus to let the Story-of-Jesus-that-goes-on-and-on in the Church shape our Story. Yes, the church's story must be freshly checked against the gospel story of Jesus, but we have no right to ignore what God has been doing in the community of Jesus since the day he sent the Spirit to empower it, ennoble it, and guide it. . . . I recommend you purchase a copy of a standard church history text, like Justo Gonzalez's highly recommended *The Story of Christianity* . . . Make a decision to know our story from Adam to the newest baptized Christian in your church. We need more of us to be curious about our ancestors. This will help us build a gospel culture.

We need also to know our creeds. . . . the wisdom of the church is on the side of the value of creeds and confessions of the faith. So I would urge you to get online, google the Apostles' Creed or the Nicene Creed, and read them. Memorize one of them if you can. (Pages 171–72, KJG)

Fourth, *we need to counter the stories that bracket our story and that reframe our story.* Our culture offers us a myriad of false stories rooted in superficial worldviews. These stories, more often than not, refuse entrance to the gospel story or reshape that gospel story or seek overtly to destroy that story. But a gospel culture can resist those stories by announcing the gospel story as the true story . . .

What are those stories?

- Individualism—the story that "I" am the center of the universe
- Consumerism—the story that I am what I own

- Nationalism—the story that my nation is God's nation
- Moral relativism—the story that we can't know what is really good
- Scientific naturalism—the story that all that matters is matter
- New age—the story that we are gods
- Postmodern tribalism—the story that all that matters is what my small group thinks

. . . We can build a gospel culture if we emphasize baptism and Eucharist as the counter stories to the cultural stories. (Pages 173–74, KJG)

Finally, we need to embrace this story so that we are saved and can be transformed by the gospel story. . . . this book is a plea that we will both discern the apostolic gospel and embrace that gospel so deeply we are wholly transformed into the image of Christ himself. A gospel culture can only be created if we are thoroughly converted ourselves. (Page 174, KJG)

We also embrace the gospel to create a gospel culture by *serving others in love and compassion.* Whether we look to the words of Jesus in the Jesus Creed of loving God and loving others, or to the words of Jesus in calling us to follow him . . . the gospel story will not leave us alone. As our God is a sending God, so we are a sent people. As our God is an other-directed God, so we are to be other-directed. The gospel propels us into mission, into the holistic mission of loving God, loving self, loving others, and loving the world. . . .

There's our gospel: it's the saving Story of Israel now lived out by Jesus, who lived, died, was buried, was raised, and was exalted to God's right hand, and who is now roaring out the message that someday the kingdom will come in all its glorious fury. (Page 176, KJG)

Reflection questions on the reading

1. What are two ways we can immerse ourselves in the story of Jesus?

2. What are two ways we can learn how the apostolic gospel has been passed down to our generation?

3. Which of the cultural stories listed in the reading is the one that appeals to you the most? Which one(s) have you wrestled with the most in trying to center your life on the Story of Jesus?

4. What does it mean to you to be others-directed, to be sent by God on a mission to love others? How might you begin to better live out being part of God's sent people?

BIBLE STUDY

As the reading points out, one of the best ways to become people of the Story of Jesus is to read the Gospels. This lesson concludes the reading of Mark's Gospel. Because your group read chapter 9 in your meeting last week, this reading picks up with chapter 10. Read chapters 10 through 16 in one sitting, either by reading or by listening to an audio Bible.

The Story of Jesus Continued (Mark 10–16)

Read Mark 10 through 16.

1. Describe your overall impression as you finished reading these chapters. How did they affect your view of Jesus?

2. Skim back through the chapters again and write down the key teachings of Jesus in these chapters.

3. After having been so immersed in Jesus' life, how did the story of his death affect you?

PRAYER

In Mark 10, Jesus asks different men in different situations the exact same question: "What do you want me to do for you?" They tell him.

In Mark 10:35–40, Jesus does not answer the request of James and John. In Mark 10:48–52, Jesus does answer the request of Bartimaeus. Why do you think Jesus answered one and not the other? How does this influence your view of prayer?

If Jesus asked you today, "What do you want me to do for you?" what would you ask him to do? Do you believe God will answer your request? Pray for something specific today that you believe is in line with God's will for you.

As you conclude your prayer time, pray the Lord's Prayer:

Our Father in heaven, hallowed be your name, your kingdom come, your will be done, on earth as it is in heaven. Give us today our daily bread. And forgive us our debts, as we also have forgiven our debtors. And lead us not into temptation, but deliver us from the evil one, for yours is the kingdom and the power and the glory forever. Amen. (Matthew 6:9–13)

ACTION

The reading mentioned the Nicene Creed. Look up a version of the creed online (there are some variations in wording) and copy it onto a full piece of paper. Stick the paper in this book because you'll need it again in a future lesson. As you write, notice what the Nicene Creed says about Jesus.

REFLECTION

In Mark 10:13–16, Jesus talks about receiving the kingdom of God like little children. Do you have children in your life, either your own or the children of family or friends? Or can you think back to when you were a child yourself?

- What do you think Jesus saw in the children that he wanted his followers to understand? What do you think it means to receive the kingdom like children? How do you think those kids felt about Jesus' attention to them and his words about them?

■ GROUP DISCUSSION ■

When your group meeting begins, say the Jesus Creed together:

Hear, O Israel, the Lord our God, the Lord is one. Love the Lord your God with all your heart, with all your soul, with all your mind, and with all your strength. The second is this: love your neighbor as yourself. There is no commandment greater than these.

The following questions are based on the personal study you already have completed. Monitor how much time your group has for discussion and answer as many of these questions together as you can.

READING

■ Look at the list of cultural stories from the reading and discuss them. Share examples from your own lives about ways those stories have shown up in your priorities or outlook.

■ How can you work to replace each of those cultural stories with the Story of Jesus?

BIBLE STUDY

■ What impressions of Jesus did you gather from the study?

■ What surprised or startled you in this Bible study?

■ If you have read any of the other Gospels, how does Mark's Gospel compare?

■ For your own continued immersion in the Story of Jesus, which gospel do you want to read next?

PRAYER

Have you ever experienced God saying no to something you have prayed for? Why do you think God didn't answer that prayer the way you would have liked?

ACTION

Watch the Bible Project video on Mark, which you can find at https://thebibleproject.com/explore/mark. (There are two—watch "Read Scripture: Mark," not "The Gospel According to Mark.")

What insights did they point out in the video that you had noticed in your own reading?

What themes and ideas did this bring out that you had not caught in your own reading?

At around the four-minute mark, the video contrasts Peter's view of "king" with Jesus' view of "king." What do the disciples mean by following King Jesus? What does Jesus mean when he asks people to follow him as king?

REFLECTION

What insights did you discover while journaling about children and the kingdom of God?

Do you have any funny or poignant stories to share about seeing children in church or about being a child in church?

If you grew up around Christianity, how has your perspective on Jesus changed as you've grown from a child to an adult?

GROUP PRAYER

Let each group member write down their prayer requests on small pieces of paper. Shuffle them and let each group member choose one—make sure not to get your own! Pray for the need on the paper you receive together in the group, then take those papers home and pray for that person several times before your next meeting. In your next group time, follow up on each other's prayer needs. Has God brought answers or resolutions?

As your group meeting ends, pray the Lord's Prayer together:

> *Our Father in heaven, hallowed be your name, your kingdom come, your will be done, on earth as it is in heaven. Give us today our daily bread. And forgive us our debts, as we also have forgiven our debtors. And lead us not into temptation, but deliver us from the evil one, for yours is the kingdom and the power and the glory forever. Amen. (Matthew 6:9–13)*

REST

As you finish these first six lessons of *Following King Jesus* on "Knowing the Gospel," flip back through the workbook and think about what has impacted you the most over the past six weeks. Then take some time to do "nothing"—let your mind wander wherever it likes as your subconscious processes everything you've learned. Give your thoughts a chance to settle and organize themselves.

PART 2

READING THE
GOSPEL

Scot and his wife, Kris, are bird watchers. They really are, not just as a reason for an occasional walk in the woods or an excuse to buy expensive binoculars or leather-bound sketchbooks. They take bird watching very seriously. My seminary cohort and I were with them on a study trip in Paul's footsteps last summer, and as we walked from our tour bus toward the Roman catacombs, Scot and Kris stopped and looked up into one of those tall evergreen Italian trees. "Listen!" they said, at first to each other, but then again to us, maybe hoping to draw us into their enthusiasm. "Listen! It's a [*words I didn't understand well enough to remember, but they were very excited*]!" And they stood there watching the high branches for a glimpse of the bird while the rest of our group wandered away, more interested in the bathrooms and the gift shop.

So it's not surprising that Scot called his book about reading and applying the Bible *The Blue Parakeet*. In the book, he tells this story of his encounter with a runaway bird. Their backyard garden is full of bird feeders, and they love to observe the cardinals, goldfinches, and chickadees that visit. One summer, Scot was reading on his back porch when he saw a blue flash. He couldn't identify the bird—not a blue jay, not an indigo bunting. He finally realized it wasn't a wild bird at all; it was someone's pet blue parakeet that had escaped its cage and flown outside. The pet bird surprised Scot, and it surprised the other birds in the yard as well. Many of them flew away, startled and frightened, and hid from the visitor. He started watching the new bird and observing the backyard social ethics. Eventually, the sparrows and other local birds got used to the parakeet's presence. They returned to their normal places and settled down. The parakeet squawked differently from the other birds and it flew in strange patterns, but the sparrows allowed the parakeet to be a parakeet, and they adjusted to its presence.

Surprise visitors shake us up and can awaken questions in us. When passages in the Bible or friends who bring up tough issues confront us with startling questions, these are "blue parakeet experiences." Blue parakeet experiences, like a student asking why we don't pray for healings, or Bible passages about foot washing, cause us to stop and think, "Is this passage for today or not?"

With the blue parakeet in his yard, Scot could have shooed it away or tried to capture it or ignored it and hoped it would go away. Instead, he observed. These are our options when we have blue parakeet experiences with the Bible: we can push them away, ignore them, try to cage them, or we can watch and learn. They can make us uncomfortable, like the parakeet made the sparrows, but we can let the Bible be the Bible, and we can adapt to it.

> There are enough passages in the Bible—and I began to sense this when I was a young Christian—that, when we read them, make us think all over again about how we are reading the Bible. I call these passages the "blue parakeet passages."
>
> Blue parakeet passages are oddities in the Bible that we prefer to cage and silence rather than to permit into our sacred mental gardens. If we are honest, blue parakeet passages often threaten us, call into question our traditional way of reading the Bible, and summon us back to the Bible to rethink how we read the Bible. (Page 262, BP)

Scot's book *The Blue Parakeet* was a blue parakeet experience for me—captivating and freeing at the same time. It was my first introduction to his work. When I read it four years ago, it reshaped my view of the Bible. It answered some of my questions, but it raised more questions than it answered, and it certainly got my mental wheels turning (which I think was the point). It inspired my curiosity and started me on a path that remodeled my understanding of my call to ministry and ultimately led me to Scot's classroom at Northern Seminary.

And that's how I found myself on the nighttime streets of Rome, a few days after the bird-in-the-tree moment, walking past a street artist who was painting galaxies on cardboard in front of the yellow glow of the Colosseum. A man stepped into my path, but what startled me more than his sudden appearance was the bird perched on his finger: a blue parakeet.

I'm pretty sure that the only place less expected to find a blue parakeet than the McKnights' backyard is a crowded sidewalk in the Forum, right where Phoebe might have walked when she delivered Paul's letter to the Roman house churches. I laughed with delight at the surprise as the man transferred his bird to my hand, then coaxed it to jump on my head. I waved to my classmates. "Take a picture!"

"He's going to charge you for it!" Josh warned me.

I was still laughing as I pulled ten euros out of my wallet. "I don't care!" That picture of me grinning and pointing at a blue parakeet on my head, surrounded by ruins and traffic, is my favorite souvenir from the trip.

The focus of these next six lessons is ultimately about figuring out "How do we live out the Bible today?" The first key takeaway is an overview of the Story of the Bible to help us file all the various verses and chapters and books into their proper places. Scot tells the Story of the Bible in three chapters, a progression from Theocracy (when God ruled the people directly) to Monarchy (when God ruled through human kings) to Christocracy (when Jesus fulfills the story as the ruling King). The second key takeaway is a set of principles for reading the Bible so that we can interpret it and apply it to our lives as we follow King Jesus. Blue parakeets will startle and confuse and delight us at the most unexpected moments along the way.

LESSON 7

WHAT IS THE BIBLE?

■ PERSONAL STUDY ■

READING

As you begin your discipleship time today, say the Jesus Creed out loud:

Hear, O Israel, the Lord our God, the Lord is one. Love the Lord your God with all your heart, with all your soul, with all your mind, and with all your strength. The second is this: love your neighbor as yourself. There is no commandment greater than these.

Pre-reading question:

1. How would you explain the Bible to someone who has never heard of it?

The Bible . . . is the creation of God, who is the Artist, and the Artist stands next to us as we read the Bible. I sometimes think we forget what we are reading. The Bible is *God's* story. When I say this, I am making a claim so extraordinary we may be tempted to skip over it. The Bible, so we believe, is unlike all other books because these words are *God's* words, this book is *God's* book, and this story is *God's* story. The overarching King and His Kingdom Story with its inner story of redemption is *God's* story and *God's* redemption.

Knowing that the Bible is God's story and that God stands next to us as we read it leads to an important question: How do we read a story that we claim is *God's* story? To dig deeper than these questions, we need to ask a better one: What is my *relationship* to the Bible? This question is one of the most important questions we can ask about reading the Bible, and I am a little startled that so many who talk about the Bible skip over the question. Too many stop short by asking only, "How can I learn to understand the Bible?"

But even that question is not good enough. The real question at the bottom of all of them is this: "What is my relationship to the *God* of the Bible?" Our relationship is not so much with the Bible but with the *God* of the Bible. There's a difference that makes a big difference. (Pages 93–94, BP)

A relational approach . . . focuses on the Bible as *God's written communication with us*. The Bible is like a spoken message or a letter from God addressed to God's people, not unlike the words we might speak or write in order to communicate something to someone we love. Once again, we must pause briefly to consider what we are saying. God is not the Bible. To make the Bible into God is idolatrous.

The Bible is God's communication—in the form of words—with us. We can trot out all the important words about the Bible—inspiration, revelation, truth, etc. But those are not enough. Behind all of these words is the astounding claim we Christians make: the Bible is God's communication with us in the form of words. For the papered book to be what it is intended to be, God's communication with us, we need to receive those words as God's words addressed to God's people. (Pages 98–99, BP)

I bring it all together into one central focus now: A relational approach believes *our relationship to the Bible is transformed into a relationship with the God who speaks to us in and through the Bible*. We come back now to our first observation: If we distinguish God from the Bible, then we also learn that in listening to God's words in the Bible, we are in search of more than a relationship with words on paper; we are seeking a relationship with the person who speaks on paper. *Our relationship to the Bible is actually a relationship with the God of the Bible*. We want to emphasize that we don't ask what the Bible says; we ask what God says to us in that Bible. The difference is a difference between paper and person.

. . . Let me now put this one final way: God gave the Bible not so we can know *it* but so we can know and love God through *it*. (Pages 100–101, BP)

Reflection questions on the reading

1. When have you heard someone ask, or when have you asked yourself, "What does the Bible say about (some topic)?" If you reframe your question from "what does the Bible say?" to "what does God say through the Bible?", how does that lead you to a more relational approach to Bible reading?

2. What do you think of the claim, "To make the Bible into God is idolatrous"? This has been called "bibliolatry"—worshipping or idolizing the Bible. How can a relational approach to the Bible keep us from bibliolatry?

3. Look above to the pre-reading question. After having done the reading and reflection, what, if anything, would you change about how you would explain the Bible to someone who has never heard of it?

BIBLE STUDY

The Delightful Words (Psalm 119)

As a college student, one of my favorite chapters of the Bible was Psalm 119. Why? Because the psalmist and I shared something: we both loved God's Word, and we both loved to study its words. But the psalmist's approach to his Bible . . . is not expressed like this: "Your words are authoritative, and I am called to submit to them." Instead, his approach is more like this: "Your words are delightful, and I love to do what you ask." The difference between these two approaches is enormous. One of them is a relationship to the Bible; the other is a relationship with God. (Page 95)

Here is perhaps the entire psalm in one line: "I have sought your face with all my heart" (v. 58). God's face! How cool is that? A relational approach to the Bible finds room for words like "delight" and "my soul is consumed" and "counselors" and "freedom" and "love" and the "theme of my song" and "good" and "precious" and "sweet" and "wonderful." (Page 96, BP)

Read Psalm 119 (yes, the whole thing).

1. Describe your overall impression as you finished reading this long psalm (it is the chapter in the Bible with the most verses). What thoughts came to mind? What did it cause you to feel?

2. Skim through the psalm and write down every different term and idea the psalmist uses for the Scriptures (for example, in verses 105–8, the psalmist uses "word," "lamp," "light," "rules," and "promise").

3. Which words does the psalmist use most frequently? Circle them in your list above.

4. Look for verses that show the psalmist's relationship with God, not just the psalmist's relationship with the Scriptures. For example, "I seek you with all my heart" (verse 10). List at least three here.

PRAYER

Psalm 119 is divided into sections, and each one is named with a letter of the Hebrew alphabet. Choose two of the lettered sections of Psalm 119 and read them out loud as a prayer of longing to know and to delight in the God of the Bible.

As you conclude your prayer time, pray the Lord's Prayer:

> *Our Father in heaven, hallowed be your name, your kingdom come, your will be done, on earth as it is in heaven. Give us today our daily bread. And forgive us our debts, as we also have forgiven our debtors. And lead us not into temptation, but deliver us from the evil one, for yours is the kingdom and the power and the glory forever. Amen. (Matthew 6:9–13)*

ACTION

Choose a verse from Psalm 119 that resonates with your desire to know God through the Bible. Write it out and post it somewhere you will see it every day this week. This can be as simple as scribbling it on a Post-it note or as complex as writing in calligraphy on special paper or creating a piece of art with the words.

REFLECTION

- Try writing your own psalm of relationship with the God of the Bible. This could take the form of a poem or song lyrics or prose. How do you view God's words to you in the Bible? What do they mean to you? How do you want them to influence your life? What words describe your longing for God to speak to you?

▪ GROUP DISCUSSION ▪

When your group meeting begins, say the Jesus Creed together:

Hear, O Israel, the Lord our God, the Lord is one. Love the Lord your God with all your heart, with all your soul, with all your mind, and with all your strength. The second is this: love your neighbor as yourself. There is no commandment greater than these.

The following questions are based on the personal study you already have completed. Monitor how much time your group has for discussion and answer as many of these questions together as you can.

READING

▪ How do each of you view the Bible?

▪ How would you explain the Bible to someone who has never read it?

▪ How did your answers to that question change between the pre-reading question and the post-reading reflection questions?

BIBLE STUDY

▪ Compare your lists of synonyms and metaphors for Scripture found in Psalm 119. Which ones did you like the most?

▪ What overall sense did reading the psalm give you?

PRAYER

As you prayed this week, did you experience any shifts in your relationship with God? How did your perspective on the Bible change and grow as you prayed about delighting in it?

ACTION

1. There is an old German Jewish tradition to start a student's schooling with an exercise of licking honey off of a writing slate, teaching them that learning Scripture is as sweet as honey. Your group facilitator could get small slates or blackboards at a craft store, one for each person in your group. The group members can write "Psalm 119" on their board with a chalk pen. Pour a little bit of honey on each board. As someone reads Psalm 119:103 out loud, the group members can lick their boards, reminding them that the Bible is sweet like honey.
2. Psalm 119 has been set to music many times. Find one such recording online and listen to it as a group.

REFLECTION

For those who are willing, read your original psalm out loud to the group. What different approaches did the group members take toward expressing their relationship with God and the Bible?

GROUP PRAYER

Get into groups of two and take turns praying for each other to grow in your love of God and your delight in God's words found in the Bible.

As your group meeting ends, pray the Lord's Prayer together:

Our Father in heaven, hallowed be your name, your kingdom come, your will be done, on earth as it is in heaven. Give us today our daily bread. And forgive us our debts, as we also have forgiven our debtors. And lead us not into temptation, but deliver us from the evil one, for yours is the kingdom and the power and the glory forever. Amen. (Matthew 6:9–13)

REST

Studying the Bible certainly can be challenging work. If you find it to be hard work, try altering your approach to the Bible this week. Read a passage and try to experience it as a restful and rejuvenating moment of receiving loving words from someone who cares deeply about you.

8

LESSON 8

HOW ARE WE TO LIVE THE BIBLE?

> **Learning intent:** Disciples will realize that all Bible readers pick and choose how to live out the Bible today and that we need to learn patterns of discernment in order to wisely adopt and adapt.
>
> **Spiritual formation intent:** Disciples will consider whether following King Jesus is a way of life that provides clear, easy answers or whether it involves wrestling with possibilities and learning to use discernment.

 **PERSONAL STUDY**

READING

As you begin your discipleship time today, say the Jesus Creed out loud:

Hear, O Israel, the Lord our God, the Lord is one. Love the Lord your God with all your heart, with all your soul, with all your mind, and with all your strength. The second is this: love your neighbor as yourself. There is no commandment greater than these.

> Throughout [my] process of conversion and reading the Bible, I made discoveries that created a question that disturbed me and still does. Many of my fine Christian friends, pastors, and teachers routinely made the claim that they were Bible-believing Christians, and they were committed to the whole Bible, and that—and this was one of the favorite lines—"God said it, I believe it, that settles it for me." They were saying two things, and I add my response (which expresses my disturbance):

One: We believe everything the Bible says, therefore . . .
Two: We *practice* whatever the Bible says.
Three: Hogwash!

Why say "hogwash," a tasty, salty word I learned from my father? Because I was reading the same Bible they were reading, and I observed that, in fact—emphasize that word "fact"—whatever they were claiming was not in "fact" what they were doing. (Nor was I.)

. . .What I learned was an uncomfortable but incredibly intriguing truth: Every one of us adopts the Bible and (at the same time) adapts the Bible, to our culture. In less appreciated terms, I'll put it this way: Everyone picks and chooses. I know this sounds out of the box and off the wall for many, but no matter how hard we try to convince ourselves otherwise, it's true. We pick and choose. (It's easier for us to hear "we adopt and adapt," but the two expressions amount to the same thing.)

I believe many of us want to know why we pick and choose. Even more importantly, many of us want to know how to do this in a way that honors God and embraces the Bible as God's Word for all times. (Page 11, 13, BP)

HOW, THEN, ARE WE TO LIVE OUT THE BIBLE TODAY?

This question never has been and never will be adequately answered with: The Bible says it, and that settles it for me. Why? Because no one does everything the Bible says. Perhaps you expected this question: How, then, are we to apply the Bible today? That's a good question. I think the word "apply" is a bit clinical and not as dynamic as the phrase "live out." (Pages 11–12, BP)

One of the themes we will encounter in this book can be summed up like this:

God spoke in Moses's days in Moses's ways, and
God spoke in Job's days in Job's ways, and
God spoke in David's days in David's ways, and
God spoke in Solomon's days in Solomon's ways, and
God spoke in Jeremiah's days in Jeremiah's ways, and
God spoke in Jesus' days in Jesus' ways, and
God spoke in Paul's days in Paul's ways, and
God spoke in Peter's days in Peter's ways, and
God spoke in John's days in John's ways,
and we are called to discern how God is carrying on that pattern in the world today.
(Pages 27–28, BP)

So how do we apply the Bible to our lives? How do we live out the story of the Bible today? Do we open up a passage, read it, and live it just as it says? Most will admit that it's not that easy, at least not all the time. (Page 125, BP)

Essentially, the church has always taught that the *times have changed and we have learned from New Testament patterns of discernment what to do and what not to do.* Often it is easy; sometimes we have to have a discussion but can agree. Other times it gets difficult. (Page 128, BP)

I have no serious desire . . . to observe all of Moses's laws "to a T." And I suspect 99.99 percent of you, if not more, stand alongside me in my lack of desire to do so. But I am quite willing to say that most of us do want to follow Jesus. Many of us, in fact, claim we do apply Jesus' teachings, literally to some degree, to everything we do.

Why talk about this? Because it is the *claim* that we follow Jesus alongside the obvious reality *that we don't follow Jesus completely* that leads us to *ponder how we are actually reading the Bible.* The passages we don't follow are blue parakeets that make us rethink how we read the Bible. . . .

. . . we don't follow Jesus literally, we do pick and choose what we want to apply to our lives today, and I want to know what methods, ideas, and principles are at work among us for picking what we pick and choosing what we choose. It is my belief that *we—the church—have always read the Bible in a picking-and-choosing way. Somehow, someway, we have formed patterns of discernment that guide us. The deepest theme in our discernment is that we have a Great Tradition—a set of methods and beliefs and a culture that holds them together—that gives us instinct for knowing how to read the Bible.* (Pages 132–33, BP)

Reflection questions on the reading

1. How have you seen someone claim to follow the Bible's teachings while you know they don't obey everything that the Bible seems to teach? How has this occurred in your own life?

2. How would you answer the big question Scot posed in the excerpt: How, then, are we to live out the Bible today?

3. So far in your journey of following King Jesus, how have you noticed that you "pick and choose" or "adopt and adapt" which Bible teachings to practice?

BIBLE STUDY

The Law (Leviticus 19)

> These . . . commands [in Leviticus 19] are never part of a discipleship program; yet they are commanded by God in the Bible. Furthermore, it's not like Moses is just giving a few good suggestions for special students who want to imitate him. In fact, these commandments are propped up with a profoundly theological comment—"I am the Lord your God." And they all start with an even more profound comment: "because I, the Lord your God, am holy." Moses anchors these commands in the holiness of God. Since God's holiness doesn't change, doesn't it make sense to think God's rules for his people don't change either?
>
> The quick answer to this question is that while God's holiness doesn't change, his will for his people does. This, then, leads to one of my favorite questions: How do we know which of those commandments change and which ones don't? How do we choose? Who gets to choose? When is there to be conservation and when is there to be innovation? (Page 127, BP)

Read Leviticus 19.

1. Make a list of all the separate commands given in this chapter.

2. Go back through your list above and underline the ones you practice in your life.

3. Go back through your list above and circle the commands that seem to have no bearing on your life.

4. Answer Scot's question: *How do we know which of those commandments change and which ones don't?*

PRAYER

Think about Leviticus 19:2: "I, the LORD your God, am holy." Focus on this verse as you pray today. The Hebrew idea of holiness is about being special or set apart—not ordinary. Honor God's holiness as you talk with God.

As you conclude your prayer time, pray the Lord's Prayer:

> *Our Father in heaven, hallowed be your name, your kingdom come, your will be done, on earth as it is in heaven. Give us today our daily bread. And forgive us our debts, as we also have forgiven our debtors. And lead us not into temptation, but deliver us from the evil one, for yours is the kingdom and the power and the glory forever. Amen. (Matthew 6:9–13)*

ACTION

Leviticus 19:10 commands farmers and harvesters to leave food in the fields at the edges for the poor and the immigrant. Do some research today to find out more about poor and immigrant people in your community. What are their challenges? What organizations already exist to help them?

- Just as farmers could provide for the poor by sharing their crops, how can you help poor and immigrant people in your area by using your professional skills, hobbies, or resources? What is a way you could adopt and adapt God's care for poor and immigrant people in your town? Make a list of ideas.

REFLECTION

Do you feel frustrated in working through this lesson? If so, how does it bring up more questions than answers? Do you tend to want religion to provide answers for all your questions? If so, how? Do you feel comfortable with mystery and uncertainty? If so, why? Set a timer for ten minutes and journal your thoughts on these questions.

▪ GROUP DISCUSSION ▪

When your group meeting begins, say the Jesus Creed together:

Hear, O Israel, the Lord our God, the Lord is one. Love the Lord your God with all your heart, with all your soul, with all your mind, and with all your strength. The second is this: love your neighbor as yourself. There is no commandment greater than these.

The following questions are based on the personal study you already have completed. Monitor how long your group has for discussion time and answer as many of these questions together as you can.

READING

▪ Discuss your faith backgrounds, whether you grew up religious or not. What observations did you make about Christians around you, whether in your church or in culture?

▪ How did various groups follow or not follow the Bible literally?

▪ Did their actions match their words about how much they valued the Bible and claimed to obey it?

▪ How do you try to live out the Bible today?

BIBLE STUDY

▪ What did each of you think was the strangest command in Leviticus 19?

■ Which ones made sense, and which ones were confusing?

PRAYER

As you prayed, how did your understanding or appreciation of God's holiness grow?

ACTION

1. Share your research about the needs of poor and immigrant people in your community. Does anyone in your group have experience connecting with people in need in your town? If so, describe the experience. Discuss what your group might be able to do to serve poor and/or immigrant people around you. Serving others together could be a valuable spiritual growth step for your group as you work to truly *live out* the Bible today.
2. Look up the TED Talk by A. J. Jacobs on his book *A Year of Living Biblically*. Watch it together as a group. Discuss: If you were to try a similar exercise, which commands might you try living out literally?

REFLECTION

For those who are willing, read some insights from your journals to each other. How do you view the roles of mystery and certainty in interpreting and applying the Bible?

GROUP PRAYER

Have each person share one command in the Bible that they want to understand more clearly or follow more faithfully. Each person can pray for the request of the person on their right.

As your group meeting ends, pray the Lord's Prayer together.

> *Our Father in heaven, hallowed be your name, your kingdom come, your will be done, on earth as it is in heaven. Give us today our daily bread. And forgive us our debts, as we also have forgiven our debtors. And lead us not into temptation, but deliver us from the evil one, for yours is the kingdom and the power and the glory forever. Amen. (Matthew 6:9–13)*

REST

Leviticus 19:3 commands the people to keep God's Sabbath. Do you think this is a command that we should practice today? How can you adopt and adapt observing the Sabbath this week?

9

LESSON 9

HOW SHOULD WE READ THE BIBLE?

Learning intent: Disciples will learn how to read the Bible with the Great Tradition to decide how to live out the Bible today.

Spiritual formation intent: Disciples will allow the Great Tradition to guide their biblical interpretation and application.

■ PERSONAL STUDY ■

READING

As you begin your discipleship time today, say the Jesus Creed out loud:

Hear, O Israel, the Lord our God, the Lord is one. Love the Lord your God with all your heart, with all your soul, with all your mind, and with all your strength. The second is this: love your neighbor as yourself. There is no commandment greater than these.

The church has always read the Bible in a picking-and-choosing way. This can also be called "adapt and adopt" or "conserve and innovate." Somehow we have formed patterns of discernment that guide us. What we here refer to as the Great Tradition is how the church has interpreted the Bible through its history, especially the points of creedal agreement and basics of the faith. This Great Tradition, this set of methods and beliefs and a culture that holds them together, provides the deepest theme in our discernment by giving us instincts for knowing how to read the Bible. We do more than read and apply; we read, we listen, and we (in connection with God's Spirit and God's people) discern.

There are three main ways to read the Bible: reading to retrieve, reading through tradition, and reading with tradition.

Reading to retrieve is going to the Bible to retrieve ideas and practices for today. This can be done by trying to retrieve all of it or by trying to retrieve only the essence. Retrieving all of it looks like following practices literally. If Paul says women should be silent in churches, then women should be silent. Retrieving the essence looks like retrieving what can be salvaged for our culture, allowing current culture to dictate or shape what we accept from the Bible.

Reading through tradition helps us avoid misreading the Bible, coming up with strange interpretations, and causing church splits. The Reformation put the Bible in the hands of ordinary Christians but also gave them tools to interpret it, and Christians now need the same. Understanding the history of Biblical interpretation is one way of reading through tradition.

Reading with tradition is returning to the Bible and retrieving ideas and practices PLUS respecting the Great Tradition PLUS letting the Holy Spirit renew us and speak to us in our time and in our ways. Reading with tradition is the way to learn how to live out the Bible today.

> I suggest we learn to read the Bible *with* the Great Tradition. We dare not ignore what God said to the church through the ages (as the return and retrieval folks often do), nor dare we fossilize past interpretations into traditionalism. Instead, *we need to go back to the Bible with our eyes on the Great Tradition so we can move forward through the church and speak God's Word in our days in our ways.* When we do this, *we must also be conscious of keeping our fresh speaking of God's Word in our day connected organically to the Great Tradition.* We need to go back without getting stuck (the return problem), and we need to move forward without fossilizing our ideas (traditionalism). We want to walk between these two approaches. It's not easy, but I contend that the best of the evangelical approaches to the Bible and the best way of living the Bible today is to walk between these approaches. It is a third way. (Pages 34–35, BP)

Part of reading with tradition is learning to use patterns of discernment, which means that as we read the Bible and locate each item in its place in the Story, as we listen to God speak to us in our world through God's ancient Word, we discern—through God's Spirit and in the context of our community of faith or the Great Tradition—a pattern of how to live in our world. There is diversity in the global church. Christians in different countries and cultures will discern differently how to live out the Bible in their culture. The pattern of discernment varies from age to age and from church to church and from person to person within a church. We have two options: uniformity of all in all things, or diversity in the striving for unity. Paul adapted himself to context. His goal was to further the gospel, and he would do whatever would best reach that goal. His mission stayed the same, but his methods changed. Everyone uses patterns of discernment regarding topics like slavery or justice or women in church ministries—blue parakeet passages that startle us and cause us to look more deeply.

> What we most need is not a return to the first or fourth or sixteenth or eighteenth century but a fresh blowing of God's Spirit on our culture, in our day, and in our ways. We need twenty-first-century Christians living out the biblical gospel in twenty-first-century ways. Even more, if we read the Bible properly, we will see that God never asked one generation to step back in time and live the way previous generations had. No, God spoke in each generation in that generation's ways. (Pages 28–29, BP)

Reflection questions on the reading

1. How have you seen Christians read to retrieve?

2. How have you seen Christians read through tradition?

3. How have you seen Christians read with tradition?

BIBLE STUDY

Justice

The New Testament authors read the Hebrew Scriptures, and as they applied them to the life of the church, they also incorporated the teachings of Jesus and heard from the Holy Spirit. They lived out the Scriptures in their days and in their ways. This is an example of reading with tradition. To repeat a key point from the reading, *"We need to go back to the Bible with our eyes on the Great Tradition so we can move forward through the church and speak God's Word in our days in our ways. When we do this, we must also be conscious of keeping our fresh speaking of God's Word in our day connected organically to the Great Tradition."*

1. ***Read Zechariah 7:9–10, Isaiah 1:17, and James 1:27.*** What did God say through the prophets Zechariah and Isaiah about justice? What did God say through James, the brother of Jesus, about religion? What do the verses from Zechariah, Isaiah, and James have in common?

2. **Read Proverbs 31:8–9 and Galatians 2:9–10.** What does the psalmist say about justice and poor people? How did the Jerusalem church leaders follow this priority in giving Paul and Barnabas ministry instructions?

3. **Read Jeremiah 22:15–17 and 1 John 3:16–18.** What did God say through Jeremiah about the good king Josiah (called "your father" in these verses)? What did John say to the church about how to show love? What do these passages have in common?

4. How do James, Paul, and John read through tradition to live out the Bible in their day?

PRAYER

First Corinthians 12:10 says that one of the gifts of the Holy Spirit is the ability to discern what messages are from God. As you pray today, ask God to help you discern by the Spirit as you study the Bible.

As you conclude your prayer time, pray the Lord's Prayer:

> *Our Father in heaven, hallowed be your name, your kingdom come, your will be done, on earth as it is in heaven. Give us today our daily bread. And forgive us our debts, as we also have forgiven our debtors. And lead us not into temptation, but deliver us from the evil one, for yours is the kingdom and the power and the glory forever. Amen. (Matthew 6:9–13 NIV)*

ACTION

One principle of discernment Scot describes in *The Blue Parakeet* is *growth in knowledge, scientific or otherwise*. The biblical writers assumed the earth was flat and held up on pillars (see for example 1 Samuel 2:8; Psalm 75:3). Now that science has advanced, we understand the universe differently. Google "ancient near eastern cosmology" and find a diagram of how people during Old Testament times understood and pictured the universe.

Draw it here:

REFLECTION

Think of a passage from the Bible that you have encountered that you don't know how to understand or apply today. How could reading through tradition and using patterns of discernment help you understand that passage? Set a timer for seven minutes and journal your thoughts.

▪ GROUP DISCUSSION ▪

When your group meeting begins, say the Jesus Creed together:

Hear, O Israel, the Lord our God, the Lord is one. Love the Lord your God with all your heart, with all your soul, with all your mind, and with all your strength. The second is this: love your neighbor as yourself. There is no commandment greater than these.

The following questions are based on the personal study you already have completed. Monitor how much time your group has for discussion and answer as many of these questions together as you can.

READING

▪ If you have done much Bible study before, which ways of reading the Bible mentioned in the reading have you tried (reading to retrieve, reading through tradition, reading with tradition)? Which do you prefer?

▪ What do you think of the concept of The Great Tradition?

BIBLE STUDY

Ask someone in the group to read out loud Micah 6:8.

▪ Besides the passages listed in the Bible study, can you think of other verses about what it means to show biblical justice?

▪ How can you adopt and adapt the many Bible passages about justice in order to live them out in your day and in your ways?

▓ What current situations in the world need an application of God's justice? How can you be someone who brings justice to these issues?

PRAYER

This week as you studied and prayed, how did you sense the Holy Spirit increasing your ability to discern and understand?

ACTION

If you are willing, share your drawings of the ancient Near Eastern view of the universe. Consider the *growth in knowledge* pattern of discernment. What other Bible passages or biblical ideas do you think could be understood using this pattern of discernment?

REFLECTION

- What Bible passages do you struggle to understand and apply?
- What ideas or solutions came to your mind as you journaled?
- What advice do you have for each other for working through difficult passages?

GROUP PRAYER

Share a challenge you are having reading the Bible this week. Pray for each other to receive discernment and knowledge from the Holy Spirit.

As your group meeting ends, pray the Lord's Prayer together:

> *Our Father in heaven, hallowed be your name, your kingdom come, your will be done, on earth as it is in heaven. Give us today our daily bread. And forgive us our debts, as we also have forgiven our debtors. And lead us not into temptation, but deliver us from the evil one, for yours is the kingdom and the power and the glory forever. Amen. (Matthew 6:9–13)*

REST

Take a break from *reading* the Bible and try *listening* to the Bible. Choose a passage and listen to an audio Bible, such as one from the free YouVersion app. How does listening change your experience of "reading" the Bible? Does it feel more restful?

10

LESSON 10

HOW DO WE LISTEN TO THE BIBLE?

Learning intent: Disciples will learn to listen with love to God's words in the Bible and learn to put their reading into practice through missional listening.

Spiritual formation intent: Disciples will challenge themselves to the "so that" stage of listening to the Bible: listening and learning so that they are equipped to do good works.

■ PERSONAL STUDY ■

READING

As you begin your discipleship time today, say the Jesus Creed out loud:

Hear, O Israel, the Lord our God, the Lord is one. Love the Lord your God with all your heart, with all your soul, with all your mind, and with all your strength. The second is this: love your neighbor as yourself. There is no commandment greater than these.

LOVING LISTENING

The Bible is . . . filled with examples of good and godly folks who paid attention to, absorbed, and then acted on the words of God. Abraham, Joseph, and Josiah are the first ones who come to mind for me. You may think of others. It's all about listening, the kind of listening that leads us to love God and to love others. The apostle Paul did not put the word "listen" in his list of what love is like in 1 Corinthians 13, but he would agree with any of us who join [scholar] Alan Jacobs by saying, "Love listens."

. . ."What would Bible reading look like if it were to be governed by 'the love chapter'?" I read Paul's words in 1 Corinthians 13:4–8 and see in these words a blueprint for reading the Bible. If love listens, then listening to God in the Bible will look like Paul's virtues of love. Add the word "listening" to each of these lines and see what happens.

> [Listening] love is patient;
> [Listening] love is kind.
> It does not envy,
> it does not boast,
> it is not proud.
> [Listening love] does not dishonor others,
> it is not self-seeking,
> it is not easily angered, keeps no record of wrongs.
> [Listening] love does not delight in evil but rejoices with the truth.
> It always protects, always trusts,
> always hopes, always perseveres.
> [Listening] love never fails.

Good reading is an act of love and therefore an act of listening. But good listening—good attentive listening, good loving listening—is more than gathering information. It is more than just sitting around the back porch with God as we sip tea while God tells us his story. God speaks to us for a reason—I call this "missional" listening. In brief, God tells his story so we can enter into a relationship with him, listen to him, and live out his Word in our day and in our way. (Pages 112–13, BP)

MISSIONAL LISTENING

Waterslides are long and wide and curvy and have wonderfully tanked sides. Water runs down the waterslide freely and abundantly to increase the speed of the slider. What we might not observe is that everything about a trip down the slide and into the pool of water at the bottom is determined by the slide itself. Even more important for our safety is that where we land is shaped by the slide. Without banked, steep sides, we would fly off the slide and . . . well, we'd get hurt.

Reading the Bible *with* our wise mentors is like sliding down a waterslide. The gospel is the slide, the Bible is one wall, our teachers and our Great Tradition are the other wall, and the water is the Holy Spirit. The pool at the bottom of the slide is our world. If we stay on the slide and inside the walls as we slide down, we will land in our own water world. If we knock down the walls of the slide or get too careless and tumble out of the safety of that slide, we could injure ourselves. However, observe this: our life is lived in the pool. Here's my point: God asks us to listen—attention, absorption, and action—to the gospel story and to read the Bible *with* our wise mentors who have gone before us. When we do that, we will land in the pool in our day and in our way. (Pages 118–19, BP)

God designs all biblical study to be a "useful" process that leads us to the Bible *in such a way that it creates a person who loves God and loves others*. Anything less fails to achieve why God speaks to us in the Bible. God's got a mission in giving us the Bible, and that mission is "useful."

. . . If we are committed to missional listening to God as we read the Bible, we will learn, we will be rebuked about our failures, and we will be restored. What is the outcome of this process? *Righteousness*. To be "righteous" means our minds, our wills, and our behaviors will be conformed to God's will. It means holiness, goodness, love, justice, and good works.

It takes time, but missional listening leads to righteousness. (Page 121, BP)

What are good works? Peter urged the Christians in Asia Minor to be benevolent in their cities; Paul exhorted the Roman Christians to love their neighbors as themselves; John urged his readers to walk in the light and to love one another; James reminded followers of Jesus to care for widows and orphans, to feed the hungry, and to clothe the naked. Good works are concrete responses to the needs we see in our neighbors.

I don't think any person reading this book wonders *what* good works are. The question is not what they are but whether we are doing them. This passage written by Paul in 2 Timothy 3:17 leads me to the following two conclusions—and they stare at each of us.

If you are doing good works, you are reading the Bible aright.

If you are not doing good works, you are not reading the Bible aright. (Page 122, BP)

Reflection questions on the reading

1. The reading talks about two types of listening. Fill in the blanks: _____ listening and _____ listening

2. How does love enter into the way we listen to the Bible?

3. What does missional listening mean?

4. What examples of good works does Scot reference from biblical authors in the reading?

BIBLE STUDY

The Mission of the Bible (1 Timothy 3)

The missional purpose of the Bible can be seen in 2 Timothy 3:14-17, an important passage for the Bible talking about itself (others include Psalm 19:7-13, Psalm 119, and 2 Peter 3:15-16). Scripture is given SO THAT we may be equipped for good works. Teaching begins with outcomes—what teachers want their students to know and do when they finish receiving instruction. "So that" is the Bible's outcome. Any reading of any passage in the Bible, the whole Story, that doesn't end up with the "so that" of 2 Timothy 3:17 is not complete.

Read 2 Timothy 3:14–17.

1. In verse 14, Paul tells Timothy to continue in what he has learned, and references those from whom Timothy learned. Who taught Timothy faith and the Scriptures? (See 2 Timothy 1:5.)

2. What does verse 15 say that the Scriptures are able to do?

3. What does verse 16 say that Scripture is useful for?

4. The outcome, the "SO THAT," comes in verse 17. What is the goal of the Scriptures?

PRAYER

Ask God to transform you through your study of Scripture. Open yourself up to God's wisdom for salvation, faith in Jesus, teaching, rebuke, correction, training in righteousness, and equipping for good works.

As you conclude your prayer time, pray the Lord's Prayer:

> *Our Father in heaven, hallowed be your name, your kingdom come, your will be done, on earth as it is in heaven. Give us today our daily bread. And forgive us our debts, as we also have forgiven our debtors. And lead us not into temptation, but deliver us from the evil one, for yours is the kingdom and the power and the glory forever. Amen. (Matthew 6:9–13)*

ACTION

Look on YouTube for a video with a first-person view of going down waterslides. There is also a fun music video for Ben Howard's song "Keep Your Head Up" about friends building and riding their own waterslide. Watch one or more waterslide videos, and then re-read the section of the reading about the waterslide analogy.

REFLECTION

As you reflect, try one of two options:

1. Can you recall a time you have gone on waterslides? How does that experience help you relate to the waterslide analogy? What do you think about that analogy of reading the Bible?
2. Come up with an original analogy of understanding how to listen to the Bible. What real-life experience can you relate to the various aspects of missional listening to the Bible? What represents the Holy Spirit, the Great Tradition, the world you live in, etc.?

■ GROUP DISCUSSION ■

When your group meeting begins, say the Jesus Creed together:

Hear, O Israel, the Lord our God, the Lord is one. Love the Lord your God with all your heart, with all your soul, with all your mind, and with all your strength. The second is this: love your neighbor as yourself. There is no commandment greater than these.

The following questions are based on the personal study you already have completed. Monitor how much time your group has for discussion and answer as many of these questions together as you can.

READING

■ Refer back to the reading and ask one group member to read out loud the modified passage from 1 Corinthians 13 about listening love.

■ How does this help you understand what listening love looks like?

■ What do you think about the idea of missional listening?

■ What could missional listening look like in your life?

BIBLE STUDY

■ Who in your life has been like Lois and Eunice were for Timothy? Who has taught you faith and Scripture?

■ How have you experienced the Bible equipping you for good works?

How do you understand "God-breathed" and "inspired" when it comes to the Scriptures?

PRAYER

As you meditated on God's work through Scripture, which aspects seem to be the most at work in your life (God's wisdom for salvation, faith in Jesus, teaching, rebuke, correction, training in righteousness, and equipping for good works)?

ACTION

Make a list together of good works you as a group could do that would show your love of God and love of neighbors. Choose one to do together this week.

REFLECTION

If you are willing, share your thoughts on the waterslide analogy and your own experiences of going down waterslides. Or share your original metaphors to explain missional listening to the Bible.

GROUP PRAYER

Try a different posture for group prayer this week. If you normally sit while praying, try standing or kneeling. If you normally hold hands, trying resting your hands on each other's shoulders. Change your position to something new as you pray for each other.

As your group meeting ends, pray the Lord's Prayer together:

Our Father in heaven, hallowed be your name, your kingdom come, your will be done, on earth as it is in heaven. Give us today our daily bread. And forgive us our debts, as we also have forgiven our debtors. And lead us not into temptation, but deliver us from the evil one, for yours is the kingdom and the power and the glory forever. Amen. (Matthew 6:9–13)

REST

Do you find waterslides fun? Do you enjoy normal playground slides? As you rest and observe the Sabbath this week, find the biggest slide in your area and go play on a playground. Joy and play and delight can all be part of our relationship with God and our rejuvenation.

11

HOW DO WE READ THE BIBLE AS STORY?

Learning intent: Disciples will learn that the various books of the Bible work together to help us understand the King and His Kingdom Story.

Spiritual formation intent: Disciples will look at how they fit into the story of the Bible. We are living in what Scot calls the "Christocracy" part of the Story, where Jesus Christ is King, so disciples will ask themselves to what extent they have made Jesus King in their lives.

■ PERSONAL STUDY ■

READING

As you begin your discipleship time today, say the Jesus Creed out loud:

Hear, O Israel, the Lord our God, the Lord is one. Love the Lord your God with all your heart, with all your soul, with all your mind, and with all your strength. The second is this: love your neighbor as yourself. There is no commandment greater than these.

Until we learn to read the Bible as Story, we will not know how to get anything out of the Bible for daily living. We need to read each passage in its location in the Story, and then we will see how it all fits together. And unless we read the Bible as Story, we might be tempted to make "that was then" into "it's also now." But it isn't. Times have changed. God . . . speaks in our days in our ways—and it is our responsibility to live out what the Bible says in our days. We do this by going back so we can come forward, always proceeding into our world organically connected to what is in our past. (Page 57, BP)

THE KING AND HIS KINGDOM STORY

To comprehend the Bible's King and His Kingdom Story, we have to go to the end of the Story, to the book of Revelation, to understand which direction we need to point ourselves as we navigate through the Bible itself. What we discover in Revelation 20–22 is that God's plan for creation is the kingdom of God. God's final kingdom here is called "a new heaven and a new earth" (Revelation 21:1). Descending from God's dwelling place, this new city over the new Jerusalem has a king, the Lamb of God, who is not only king but the temple itself! God will be the people's God and the people will be God's people. There is something profoundly important in beginning with the end: we see that the plan of God is not just my personal salvation . . . but all of creation's benefits! Evil will be defeated, goodness will finally be established for all time, all jewels and glittery items will be donated to the glory of God, the Lamb is all the light the new Jerusalem will need, peace and safety and open doors will be the way of life, and all God's people will worship the one true God. Knowing this end teaches us how to read the Bible's King and His Kingdom Story. I suggest there are three chapters in this Story:

Theocracy:

The Creator God who makes a covenant with Abraham rules, no humans are to rule, and all humans are to trust and obey this one true God. This Story is found from Genesis 1 to 1 Samuel 8. Thus, the story extends from Adam and Abraham to Moses and Samuel, but a noticeable feature of this story is that humans constantly resist the will of God, God makes a covenant to redeem them, gives the law to guide them, and provides a sacrificial system to reconcile them to himself. But most importantly, God turns his gracious and guiding attention especially to one family, Abraham's, and to one nation, Israel. From Genesis on, the core of the Bible's Story is Israel, and in the New Testament it is the church. Noticeably, unlike the nations all around Israel, there is no king among the one true God's people. God alone is their king.

Monarchy:

God permits, but only permits, his people Israel to have a king, a monarch. Why? Because as Samuel says to God, Israel wants a king so that they can be like the other nations. This extends from 1 Samuel 8 to Matthew 1:1. This can be called the monarchical concession of God in order to discipline Israel to see that God's original way—theocracy—is the best way. God remains the one true God and King, but Israel gets a human king who is to be under God the King. Yet again, the kings act like the humans under Theocracy: they resist the will of God; God's covenant provides a way of reconciliation and restoration; the sages of Israel develop wisdom for the people of God so they will learn how to live well and flourish; the prophets become more central to announce God's will, to predict the future, and to declare that someday God will bring Israel back into a theocracy again. In the Monarchy chapter, law, wisdom, and prophecy mature and become central to the community of God, Israel.

Christocracy:

God calls a halt to the human rule of a monarchy, sends his royal Son—Jesus the King, the Messiah, the Son of God and Son of Man, and Wisdom incarnate. He lives with us, shows us how to live, teaches us the way of God, and then he dies for us, he is buried, he is raised for us, and he ascends to the right hand of the Father to rule. The Christocracy period extends from Matthew 1:1 to the end of Revelation, where the Lamb who is the Lion who is the Son rules with the Father over the new heaven and the new earth. Once again, God rules (Christocracy is the theocracy), but now the people of God expand from Israel to include gentiles in the one people of God, the church. This people too are not perfect. Church people sin, but forgiveness is now granted through the cross of Christ. This Christocracy, the church age, will be completed when Christ returns, all evil is defeated, and the ways of God are established forever. Christocracy will then turn, as 1 Corinthians 15:20–28 shows, back into Theocracy.

This is the Bible's General Plot: from God creating the heavens and the earth to the completion of creation by establishing the new heaven and the new earth. I call this three-chapter Story the King and His Kingdom Story. This King and His Kingdom Story shapes every other story that can be told from the Bible, and stories that ignore the King and His Kingdom Story—any story where Jesus and his redemptive benefits are not central—fail to be consistent with the Bible's General Plot. (pages 68–71, BP)

Reflection questions on the reading

1. Have you ever thought about reading the Bible as a story before? Why or why not?

2. What does Scot suggest as the three chapters in the Bible's Story?

3. How does this idea of the King and His Kingdom Story shape or reshape your ideas about the Bible?

BIBLE STUDY

Stephen Tells the Story (Acts 7)

Stephen was a leader in the early church in Jerusalem. Because of his wisdom and the great and obvious gifts the Holy Spirit gave him, he was one of the people entrusted with taking practical care of the needs of the widows as the church did good works. He also did miracles by the power of the Spirit. Synagogue leaders brought false charges against him, saying he spoke against Moses and the temple. (See Acts 6 for this background information on Stephen.)

In this speech to the Sanhedrin, a Jewish council, Stephen defends himself by telling the story of the Bible as he sees it, giving special attention to Moses's story and showing that he holds orthodox beliefs about Moses and the role of that important prophet in the story of God. He throws in a mention of the temple at the end, then he brings the story to fulfillment in Jesus.

Read Acts 7:1–53.

1. Write out where you see Theocracy, Monarchy, and Christocracy in Stephen's telling of the Bible's story?

2. How does Stephen use the Old Testament Scriptures to tell a story that leads to Jesus?

Read Acts 7:54–60.

3. What happens to Stephen after he tells the story?

4. Notice verse 58, which mentions a young man named Saul. This is Saul of Tarsus who later goes by the name Paul and becomes a missionary for Jesus to the gentiles. What impact do you think Stephen's story had on Saul?

PRAYER

Take a coat or sweater out of your closet and lay it on the floor at your feet. Imagine what Saul might have seen and heard and felt as he listened to Stephen's sermon and then as he took care of the coats while he watched the older men stone Stephen to death. Ask God to impact you through Stephen's telling of the Bible's story, to transform you and help you more fully enter the story of God and God's people. Sit or kneel quietly as you try to hear what God might be saying to you. Notice any gentle challenges that come to mind encouraging you to focus on certain actions or mind-sets in your life where God wants to make you more like Jesus. If your mind wanders, focus your eyes on the coat as a way of re-centering your thoughts.

As you conclude your prayer time, pray the Lord's Prayer:

> *Our Father in heaven, hallowed be your name, your kingdom come, your will be done, on earth as it is in heaven. Give us today our daily bread. And forgive us our debts, as we also have forgiven our debtors. And lead us not into temptation, but deliver us from the evil one, for yours is the kingdom and the power and the glory forever. Amen. (Matthew 6:9–13)*

ACTION

Watch the Bible Project's five-and-a-half-minute video on the story of the Bible (https://thebibleproject.com/videos/the-story-of-the-bible/). How does their summary compare or contrast with Scot's summary?

- Think about how you would tell the story of the Bible. Jot down a bulleted list of the main points you would want to include.

Practice saying all the main points and verbally add in your transition thoughts and other details as you go.

Who do you know who would be willing to listen to you tell a short version of the Bible's story? A friend, a coworker, a child in your life, a relative? They don't have to be a Christian, and in fact, it would be more interesting if they were not. Send them a message or give them a call right now to plan a time to get together so you can practice telling this story. You could tell the story by email or text or on a phone or video call, but ideally you would do this in person. (One of your small group members doesn't count—they will likely have the chance to hear you tell the story when your group gets together this week!)

REFLECTION

Review the end of the Reading section earlier in the lesson about Chapter 3 of the Story: Christocracy. Read that paragraph out loud to yourself.

- Is Jesus Christ the actual ruler of my life? Do I see him as king? Is my life beginning to show that I live in the Christocracy chapter of the King and His Kingdom Story? Set a timer for ten minutes and try to write without stopping. Don't worry about correctness or stress over every word—just get your thoughts down on the paper.

■ GROUP DISCUSSION ■

When your group meeting begins, say the Jesus Creed together:

Hear, O Israel, the Lord our God, the Lord is one. Love the Lord your God with all your heart, with all your soul, with all your mind, and with all your strength. The second is this: love your neighbor as yourself. There is no commandment greater than these.

READING

■ Had you ever considered the Bible's story in this way?

■ Do you agree or disagree with Scot's main phases of the story?

BIBLE STUDY

■ Read Acts 7 out loud. One person can be the designated reader, or all group members can take turns reading sections or verses.

■ What stood out to you or interested you in Acts 7?

PRAYER

Talk about your experiences in prayer this week. If you are willing, share about how you are being transformed by the Bible's story, or specifically by Stephen's telling of the story.

ACTION

1. Show your group your bullet-point list of the highlights of the Bible's story. To whom did you decide to practice telling the story? Have you met with them yet? If so, how did it go?
2. The facilitator of the group can bring modeling clay or paper and markers. Each group member can shape or draw three objects to represent the three chapters of the King and His Kingdom Story: one for Theocracy, one for Monarchy, and one for Christocracy. After everyone has made their clay objects or drawn their pictures, each person can share what they made and why.

Next, group members can practice telling the Story of the Bible using their objects or drawings to remind them of the three chapters of the story.

REFLECTION

If you are willing, share something from your journaling time. What insights did you have as you wrote down your thoughts about your life lived in a Christocracy?

GROUP PRAYER

As you pray for each other this week, one person can begin by praying a short prayer for themselves or a need in their life. The next person in the circle can pray for the need of the first person, and then add a prayer for themselves. The third person prays for the second person and then themselves, and so on. The prayer ends when the first person to pray concludes by praying for the need of the last person in the circle.

As you conclude, pray the Lord's Prayer together:

> *Our Father in heaven, hallowed be your name, your kingdom come, your will be done, on earth as it is in heaven. Give us today our daily bread. And forgive us our debts, as we also have forgiven our debtors. And lead us not into temptation, but deliver us from the evil one, for yours is the kingdom and the power and the glory forever. Amen. (Matthew 6:9–13)*

REST

Make time today to set aside work. Do something you enjoy, not because it's productive, but because it refreshes you. Or do nothing at all. Remember that God is your provider, and it's healthy to take a break from working to rest and honor God.

12

LESSON 12

NOW WHAT?

> **Learning intent:** Disciples will see that studying the Bible calls them to action in their world.
>
> **Spiritual formation intent:** Disciples will tell the Bible's story to themselves and to others in ways that shape their daily lives and priorities.

■ PERSONAL STUDY ■

READING

As you begin your discipleship time today, say the Jesus Creed out loud:

Hear, O Israel, the Lord our God, the Lord is one. Love the Lord your God with all your heart, with all your soul, with all your mind, and with all your strength. The second is this: love your neighbor as yourself. There is no commandment greater than these.

> Many of us will be tempted to take shortcuts when we read the Bible and especially when we encounter a blue parakeet passage. Instead of reading each passage in its storied context, we will zoom in on getting out of the Bible what we want. (Page 262, BP)
>
> It is tempting to return to the safety of our former reading habits. But if we listen to the blue parakeet passages in the Bible, which are there at God's discretion, and if we think about how we are reading them, the Bible somehow unfolds before our eyes as a brilliant Story. (Page 263, BP)
>
> God chose to give us a collection of books, what I call wiki-stories of the Story, and together these books form God's story with us and God's story for us. . . . each author in the Bible is a wiki-storyteller and each book is then a wiki-story, one story in the ongoing development of the big story. (Page 264, BP)

Furthermore, each wiki-storyteller, each author in the Bible, tells a story that will lead us to the person of the Story: Jesus Christ. As Moses and Isaiah look forward to that person, so Paul and Peter and the author of Hebrews look back to that person. Jesus Christ, then, is the goal and the center of each wiki-story. The Theocracy worked through a Monarchy, but the whole Story was aimed at the Christocracy, the rule of the Messiah as the world's one true Lord . . .

We must never make the mistake of exalting the paper on which the Bible is written over the Person who puts the words on that paper. Our relationship to the Bible is actually, if we are properly engaged, a relationship with the God of the Bible. God gave us the Bible as a person who speaks to you and me as persons through words. God gave us the Bible so we could be transformed and bring glory to him by living out a life in this world that God designs for us. How do we do this?

We are summoned by the God who speaks to us in the Bible to *listen* to God speak, to *live out* what God directs us to live out, and to *discern how* to live out the Story in our own day. One way of saying all of this can be found in Moses's original words and in what I call the Jesus Creed version of Moses's words: we are to love God and to love others. If we love God and love others, we will listen to God in the Bible, live out what God calls us to live out, and discern how to live out the Story in our world today. (Pages 265–66, BP)

Reading the Bible as Story teaches us to look forward by looking to our past. It teaches us to go back to that story so we know how to go forward in our world. We must not be afraid of where God will lead us as we live out this story today, just as David and Isaiah and Jesus and Paul and Peter were unafraid where God might lead them. We cannot think that we will find security by going back and staying in the past. We cannot think that our task is complete once we've figured what Paul or Peter meant when they spoke of the gospel in their world. Instead, we are given a pattern of discernment in the Bible, a pattern that flows directly out of the Story, to listen to what God said in that world so we can know what God is saying to us through our world. So we can know what God wants us to say about that story to our world—in our world's ways.

If the Bible does anything for us as we read it as Story, it gives us the confidence to face the future with the good news about Jesus Christ in the power of the Spirit. God's Spirit, the Story tells us, is with us to guide us and to give us discernment.

The story of the Bible is not only the story of our past, it is the story for our future. (Pages 266–67, BP)

Reflection questions on the reading

1. Why does Scot say that God gave us the Bible?

2. What does God, through the Bible, summon us to do? (The answers are in italics in the reading.)

    - _____
    - _____
    - _____

3. After we study and try to understand and interpret the Bible, what should we do next? *Now what?*

BIBLE STUDY

Peter Tells the Story (Acts 2)

After Jesus ascended, he told his disciples to wait in Jerusalem for the Holy Spirit. The women and men who had been Jesus' friends and followers met together in the upper room and prayed. On the Feast of Pentecost, the sound of wind and the appearance of fire filled the place, and the Holy Spirit filled all the gathered disciples. They started speaking in other languages so loudly that Jews from other nations who were visiting the city for the feast heard them, understood them, and ran to find out what was going on. Peter stepped up to explain. Read how he tells a wiki-story of the Story and then explains how they are all called to live out the Story in their day.

Read Acts 2:14–40.

1. List all the passages from the Hebrew Scriptures Peter references in his sermon. Your Bible should indicate his references in some way, such as footnotes or cross reference notes.

2. How does Peter interpret and explain the Scriptures he references, through the discernment the Holy Spirit gives him? How does he point the wiki-stories to the person of the Story, Jesus?

3. In verse 38, how does Peter bring the Story around to the application for their days and their ways? What does he tell the people to do?

Read Acts 2:41–47.

4. How do the people respond to Peter's telling of the Story? List all the various actions of the new believers in response.

PRAYER

Pray about what is next for you. What is God summoning you to do as you study the Bible? How is God calling you to live out the Story of the Bible in your days and in your ways? Try to quiet your mind and spend time in silence, listening for the Holy Spirit to speak to you. If any thoughts or pictures or promptings or ideas from Scripture pop into your mind, write them down briefly, then go back to listening.

As you conclude your prayer time, pray the Lord's Prayer:

Our Father in heaven, hallowed be your name, your kingdom come, your will be done, on earth as it is in heaven. Give us today our daily bread. And forgive us our debts, as we also have forgiven our debtors. And lead us not into temptation, but deliver us from the evil one, for yours is the kingdom and the power and the glory forever. Amen. (Matthew 6:9–13)

ACTION

Reread Acts 2:41–47. Which actions of the early church do you live out today? Which ones would you like to try as a way of living out the Bible today? What are some practical ways you could take action on these ideas from the example of the first believers?

REFLECTION

The readings summarized several main ideas from *The Blue Parakeet*: blue parakeet passages, wiki-stories, reading the Bible as Story, the chapters of the Story (Theocracy, Monarchy, Christocracy), the person of the Story (Jesus), a relational approach to the God of the Bible instead of bibliolatry, using patterns of discernment to understand how to apply the Bible to our lives, and the imperative to live out the Bible today.

Which of these ideas in this section of *Following King Jesus* has most impacted your view of the Bible? Underline it in the list in the first paragraph. How has it changed your perspective? What do you do differently now as a result? Take some time to journal your answers to these questions.

▪ GROUP DISCUSSION ▪

When your group meeting begins, say the Jesus Creed together:

Hear, O Israel, the Lord our God, the Lord is one. Love the Lord your God with all your heart, with all your soul, with all your mind, and with all your strength. The second is this: love your neighbor as yourself. There is no commandment greater than these.

The following questions are based on the personal study you already have completed. Monitor how much time your group has for discussion and answer as many of these questions together as you can.

READING

How would you summarize the lessons on "Reading the Gospel"?

Look back at this lesson's reading, which is a summary of some of the ideas in *The Blue Parakeet*. What would your own summary of these lessons include or leave out that is different from this summary?

Which reading from *The Blue Parakeet* was your favorite?

BIBLE STUDY

Different Christian traditions have different perspectives on how and when believers are "filled with the Holy Spirit" and on the role of "speaking in tongues" for Christians today. What are your thoughts on these topics?

What did you think of Peter's sermon? How does it compare or contrast with sermons you have heard in churches today?

What appealed to you about the life of the very early believers? What seemed strange or uncomfortable to you?

PRAYER

If you are willing, share ideas that came to your mind as you listened to God.

ACTION

What ideas did you come up with for how you might like to try living out the Bible like the early church lived out the Scriptures and the teachings of Jesus? Which idea would your group like to do together? Plan a time and the logistics to try it.

REFLECTION

If you are willing, share thoughts from your journaling time as you reflected on these six lessons about the Bible. How do you see the Bible differently now?

GROUP PRAYER

Does anyone in your group speak a language other than English? Ask that person to pray for your group in another language. The rest of the group can agree in prayer as they listen. What is it like to hear someone pray, knowing that while you can't understand them, God does?

As your group meeting ends, pray the Lord's Prayer together:

> *Our Father in heaven, hallowed be your name, your kingdom come, your will be done, on earth as it is in heaven. Give us today our daily bread. And forgive us our debts, as we also have forgiven our debtors. And lead us not into temptation, but deliver us from the evil one, for yours is the kingdom and the power and the glory forever. Amen. (Matthew 6:9–13)*

REST

As the new believers made time to break bread together, plan a meal together with one or more other people soon. Share the work of the meal to help everyone get a bit of a break from cooking and cleaning.

PART 3

LIVING THE GOSPEL

When I was a pre-teen, my family lived on acres of wooded property in Northwest Arkansas. A few other houses dotted the hills, and after school, all the kids would gather to roam the ravines and build forts and swing on vines. When we got tired of that, I roped people into putting on elaborate dance performances in our driveways. One summer we choreographed a group dance to Steven Curtis Chapman's song "The Great Adventure." It lends itself well to being acted out with lines about saddling horses and blazing trails.

But another of Chapman's songs is the one that really stuck with me: "For the Sake of the Call." I recorded it onto a cassette tape while I was listening to the Christian radio station. Jesus' crazy call of "Follow me" cut through the rules of Christianity and gave me a glimpse of the freedom and risk of discipleship. I came across the song again recently when some friends were listening to "vintage Christian music," and it reminded me of the life of discipleship that has intrigued me since I was young girl. Chapman sings about the disciples Jesus called from a life of fishing for fish and asked them to fish for people instead. Jesus asked his disciples then, and still asks us today, to abandon everything else in life in order to follow him. I encourage you to go find the lyrics and the song by Steven Curtis Chapman on the internet and listen carefully to the words.

Some days I wrestle with this "yoke" of following Jesus, and it doesn't feel as light as he said it would be. Some days I really don't want to be like Jesus, because his way is hard. It's unnatural. I'm a fighter like Peter. I'm arrogant and sharp-tongued like Paul. I'm a know-it-all like Martha. I'm full of thunder like John. Being kind to people who are cruel to me isn't normal. Forgiving instead of getting revenge isn't easy.

But as those disciples followed Jesus, his example and his Spirit changed them. Peter became tempered in his boldness. Paul became humble. Martha became a servant and a declarer of the Messiah. John became self-giving. I'm trusting Jesus to keep changing me too. I'll never be done learning from him—my older brother and friend, my teacher and liberator, my king. On the hard discipleship days, I find myself wondering if I can keep following Jesus, then saying with Peter, "Where else would I go? You have the words of life." I'm going to keep answering that call.

Scot answered that same call. He shares his early Christian life in his book *One.Life*.

I want to draw your attention to what [my] first two lessons in life taught me:

A Christian is someone who has accepted Jesus; and the Christian life is the development of personal (private) practices of piety, separation from sin and the world, and a life dedicated to rescuing sinners from hell.

. . . I learned to define who I was by a single-moment act, and by what I did and what I didn't do. I knew I was a Christian, because I had accepted Christ and I was doing the right things—and not doing the wrong things.

This single-moment decision plus personal practices of piety is one answer to the question, and I'll get to the question in a minute. Before we get there, I want to observe that Jesus didn't focus on the single-moment act as much as we did, and neither did he frame "the Christian life" with anything quite like these practices. I have to put "Christian life" in quotes because he framed such a thing more in terms of discipleship. . . .

Every time the single-moment act of accepting Christ becomes the goal instead of the portal, we get superficial Christians. And every time personal practices of piety wiggle away from the big picture Jesus sketches before his followers, it becomes legalism. And I became a legalist. . . . Every time we get too focused on the single-moment act or our personal practices of piety, we wander into legalism and then we lose Jesus. I lost him in the middle of doing very good (mostly Christian) things.

I realize I haven't even told you what I think the question is, but I'm about to. There are different answers to this question, and it all depends on where you begin. *One.Life* seeks to answer the question by examining what Jesus says, so now I'll reveal the question and provide a quick answer . . .

The question: *What is a Christian?*

Answer: *A Christian is someone who follows Jesus.*

My former answer: *A Christian is someone who has accepted Jesus, and the Christian life focuses on*

personal practices of piety. (Pages 13–15, OL)

Now in my third decade of studying and teaching the Gospels, I want to sketch how Jesus understood what we call "the Christian life." If we were to ask Jesus our question—*What is a Christian?*—what would he say? . . . Jesus' answer, which he stated a number of times, was, "Follow me." Or, "Become my disciple."

But what does that look like? . . . I want to sketch Jesus' vision of what it means to be one of his followers. I'm about to suggest to you that the Bible.Reading.Praying.Going-to-Church. Evangelizing approach is not enough. I'm going to suggest that Jesus focused on other things and, as we do the same, each of these other items takes its place as a means to Jesus' bigger ideas. Instead of a personal-practices-of-piety plan, Jesus offers to us a *kingdom-holiness* plan. Jesus offers to us a *kingdom dream* that can transform us to the very core of our being.

His vision is so big we are called to give our entire lives to it.

His vision is so big it swallows up our dreams. (Page 17, OL)

13

LESSON 13

KINGDOM LIFE

> **Learning intent:** Disciples will learn what Jesus' contemporaries heard when Jesus said "kingdom."
> **Spiritual formation intent:** Disciples will seriously consider what role God is calling them to play in blessing all people by bringing the good news of God's kingdom.

■ PERSONAL STUDY ■

READING

As you begin your discipleship time today, say the Jesus Creed out loud:

Hear, O Israel, the Lord our God, the Lord is one. Love the Lord your God with all your heart, with all your soul, with all your mind, and with all your strength. The second is this: love your neighbor as yourself. There is no commandment greater than these.

> Jesus was a Dream Awakener. He startled his contemporaries from their self-imposed deep sleep by standing up tall and in front of everyone and announcing the following three lines:
>
> *The time has come.*
> *The kingdom of God has come near.*
> *Repent and believe the good news!*
> . . .
>
> For Jesus the word *kingdom* meant "God's dream for this world come true." But we need to get our minds and hearts and bodies around one very important element of this word *kingdom*:

Kingdom wasn't just Jesus' dream, but the dream of everyone in Israel. Pick up any of Israel's Prophets in the Old Testament, like the long and winding Isaiah or the short and abrupt Haggai, and you will catch snippets of a bold and robust hope for what God would do someday. Jesus was capturing those dreams when he announced the time had now come. Jesus is the Dream Awakener when he uses this term. (Page 28, OL)

When they heard the word "kingdom," what do you think the contemporaries of Jesus imagined?

Every Jew in Galilee and everywhere else, and I mean every one of them, when they heard Jesus say "the kingdom," looked for three things: king, land, citizens. This might surprise you, but that is only because so many Christians have turned kingdom into either a "personal experience with Jesus" (the evangelical meaning of kingdom) or into "cultural redemption" (the liberal, progressive meaning of kingdom). When Jesus said "kingdom," the first thing his hearers looked for was a king, and then they were thinking of the land (or a sacred place or sacred space) and themselves as participants (citizens). This needs to be fleshed out for one reason: Kingdom is not about an experience with God but about the society of God, and this society is Jewish (and biblical) to the core.

First, especially if you are a first-century Jew, kingdom means there is a *king*. . . . That means goodbye to the Roman presence and goodbye to the corrupt, mixed-heritage local kings like Herod Antipas. Another word for *king* in Jesus' Jewish world—and I'm not sure Christians think of this as quickly as they should—is *Messiah*. When Jesus claims the kingdom has arrived, there is an immediate correlation of high blood pressure for the Herodians and heart-pounding joy for the Galilean peasants who know their day has (finally) arrived. Next, every one of Jesus' contemporaries connects kingdom to the *land* where the king exercises his kingly rule. The contemporaries of Jesus know the Messiah will sit atop a throne in Jerusalem and rule the land. They know the land will flow with milk and honey and grapes (good ones, as at the wedding in Cana) and everyone will own a plot of that land and they will all have good crops and good neighbors and they will all follow the Torah. Finally, every Jewish listener thought of the *citizens* who love the King and who serve the King and who work for the King and his kingdom in the land of Israel. On top of this, as is known from the first promises to Abraham through the whole of the Bible, Israel had a mission to bless the nations, and Jesus was summoning his disciples to become that blessing.

We need to shed our unearthly and nonsocial and idealistic and romantic and uber-spiritual visions of kingdom and get back to what Jesus meant. By kingdom, Jesus means: *God's Dream Society on earth, spreading out from the land of Israel to encompass the whole world*. In our terms today, Jesus was ultimately talking about the Church as the partial and imperfect manifestation of the kingdom of God. What this means is so important: When Jesus was talking about the kingdom of God, he was thinking of concrete realities on the earth, he was thinking of the Church being the embodiment of the Jesus dream, and he was thinking of you and me living together in a community as we should. (Pages 30–31, OL)

Kingdom is an interconnected society;
Kingdom is a society noted by caring for others;
Kingdom is a society shaped by justice;
Kingdom is a society empowered by love;
Kingdom is a society dwelling in peace;
Kingdom is a society flowing with wisdom;
Kingdom is a society that knows its history;
Kingdom is a society living out its memory;
Kingdom is a society that values society;
Kingdom is a society that cares about its future.

This is what I think we miss when we turn kingdom into personal and private spirituality: Jesus chose one of the most social terms he could find to express what God was now doing. Jesus didn't choose "personal relationship with God" but instead he chose the term *kingdom*. He did so because his dream was of a kingdom on earth, a society where God's will flowed like rivers of good wine.

This understanding of kingdom is at the center of everything I learned and everything I've been teaching. If you want to know how Jesus understands the Christian life, the place to begin is with what he means by kingdom of God. That's where Jesus himself began. So the first line I'd add to answer our question is this:

A Christian is someone who follows Jesus by devoting his or her One.Life to the kingdom vision of Jesus. (Page 34, OL)

Reflection questions on the reading

1. Before doing the reading, what did you think when you heard the phrase "kingdom of God"?

2. According to the reading, what are the three elements of "kingdom"?

3. What does the reading say Jesus means when he says "kingdom"?

BIBLE STUDY

The Land, the People, and the King (Genesis 12 and 18; Galatians 3)

Read Genesis 12:1–7.

1. What did God promise Abraham? List all the elements of the promise.

2. What do these verses say would be the global impact of God's commitment to Abraham?

Read Genesis 18:17–19.

3. What condition did God place on the promise to Abraham? (Abraham will do _____ so that God will do _____.)

Read Galatians 3:7–9, 14, 28–29.

4. How does Paul explain the fulfilment of God's promise to Abraham in Paul's days?

PRAYER

Are there dreams or promises God has given you that you have not seen fulfilled? God was still working on fulfilling the promise to Abraham thousands of years later during the New Testament period, and God is still blessing the whole world through the promise thousands more years later today. Ask God to increase your faith as you wait for him to make good on your God-given dreams.

As you conclude your prayer time, pray the Lord's Prayer:

> *Our Father in heaven, hallowed be your name, your kingdom come, your will be done, on earth as it is in heaven. Give us today our daily bread. And forgive us our debts, as we also have forgiven our debtors. And lead us not into temptation, but deliver us from the evil one, for yours is the kingdom and the power and the glory forever. Amen. (Matthew 6:9–13)*

ACTION

Missionaries spend their vocational lives fulfilling the mission of Israel that becomes the mission of all God's people in Jesus: blessing all nations by inviting them to join the kingdom of God.

Choose one of these missionaries and do some research on them. How did they live out the mission?

- Amy Wilson Carmichael
- Gladys Aylward
- Betsey Stockton

REFLECTION

Do you live your life in such a way that you are a blessing to people? How can you do a better job of living to bring God's blessing and God's community and God's good news to the people around you? How can you live out the mission of Abraham and Israel and Jesus and Paul today?

■ GROUP DISCUSSION ■

When your group meeting begins, say the Jesus Creed together:

Hear, O Israel, the Lord our God, the Lord is one. Love the Lord your God with all your heart, with all your soul, with all your mind, and with all your strength. The second is this: love your neighbor as yourself. There is no commandment greater than these.

The following questions are based on the personal study you already have completed. Monitor how much time your group has for discussion and answer as many of these questions together as you can.

READING

■ Discuss the possible reactions of Jesus' contemporaries when they heard him talk about the kingdom. How do you think the different types of people who heard him felt and responded?

BIBLE STUDY

■ Think back to the previous lesson on reading the Bible as Story. How do you see the Bible's Story running through the Bible study this week? How do the passages you read fit into the bigger narrative?

PRAYER

If you are willing, share the dreams and promises God has given you. How do you feel about waiting patiently for their fulfillment? If God has brought a dream to life for you, share that as well.

ACTION

Look up and take turns reading out loud the points in this article about how South Korean churches have been so successful in sending missionaries: https://www.imb.org/2018/02/09/south-korea-mission-movement/

How could your group or church adopt some of these ideas to prepare, motivate, and send out more people to preach the good news of the kingdom?

REFLECTION

- What is God stirring in your heart about becoming more involved in God's global mission?
- What steps will you take toward that goal?
- How can the group help you and support you?

GROUP PRAYER

Let each group member pray for a people group somewhere in the world who needs to hear the good news of God's kingdom. Pray for God to send willing workers to that area.

As your group meeting ends, pray the Lord's Prayer together:

Our Father in heaven, hallowed be your name, your kingdom come, your will be done, on earth as it is in heaven. Give us today our daily bread. And forgive us our debts, as we also have forgiven our debtors. And lead us not into temptation, but deliver us from the evil one, for yours is the kingdom and the power and the glory forever. Amen. (Matthew 6:9–13)

REST

Do an activity that relaxes you and doesn't take much thought or attention. Let your mind wander as you meditate on this thought: "Is my life devoted to God's kingdom?"

14

LESSON 14

LOVE LIFE

Learning intent: Disciples will learn the two greatest commandments.

Spiritual formation intent: Disciples will work on applying Jesus' most important instructions in their lives as they seek to love God and love others.

■ PERSONAL STUDY ■

READING

As you begin your discipleship time today, say the Jesus Creed out loud:

Hear, O Israel, the Lord our God, the Lord is one. Love the Lord your God with all your heart, with all your soul, with all your mind, and with all your strength. The second is this: love your neighbor as yourself. There is no commandment greater than these.

For Jesus, everything is shaped toward becoming people who love God and who love others, and nothing less than a life absorbed in love is sufficient to describe what a Christian is for him. Any accepting of Jesus and all pious practices is designed to make us people who love God and who love others. (Page 47, OL)

Jesus was deconstructive and constructive, and that is why he took his followers on a journey into the core of what God's Dream Society was about: the Love.Life. (Page 49, OL)

By the time of Jesus it was common knowledge that the Torah contained 613 separate commands and prohibitions. Add to those all the rulings (*halakot*) and you've got lots to learn and lots of help to make sure you know how to live the 613. All designed to help ordinary people "do Torah" well. Or at least that was the plan.

Not everyone agreed that this was how to make the Torah doable. Including Jesus. (Page 50, OL)

Jesus found a new way, a better way. Instead of obeying the 613 by adding rulings that helped clarify the specifics, no matter how valuable those specifics might be, Jesus reduced the 613 . . . TO TWO.

Jesus revealed that the number two was the guide to the number 613. One of these religious experts came to Jesus, because he wanted to trap Jesus in a theological debate. (Or, in our terms, because he wanted Jesus to tell the crowd which denomination he was in or whose side he was on in a political or religious debate.) In Mark's twelfth chapter, the scribe asks this in verse 28: "Of all the commandments [the 613], which is the most important?" If Jesus picks one, he could be guilty of picking and choosing the wrong one. If he doesn't pick one, he looks lame. Jesus was ready and his answer deconstructed the entire "613 plus *halakot*" approach to the Torah, and he offers to his listeners in verses twenty-nine to thirty-one what I call the Jesus Creed:

> "The most important one," answered Jesus, "is this: 'Hear, O Israel: The Lord our God, the Lord is one. Love the Lord your God with all your heart and with all your soul and with all your mind and with all your strength.' The second is this: 'Love your neighbor as yourself.' There is no commandment greater than these."
>
> *Mark 12:29–31*

Or, as Matthew 22:40 finishes off this very same exchange:

> "All the Law and the Prophets hang on these two commandments."

What Jesus said to the [religious] of his day was this: You are fixated on your *love of Torah* and judging others by whether or not they live up to your standards and your rulings, but what you must understand is that God gave us a *Torah of love*.

What God really wants is for you and me to love God and to love others, and if we do that everything else will fall in line. Jesus' words are mind-blowing and they initiate us into his grand vision of the kingdom of God. The 613 aren't understood until you understand that every commandment is either a "love God" or a "love your neighbor" command. To turn these two into 613 is to minimize the centrality of love. To see the 613 as expressions of either loving God or loving others is to set the 613 free to be what God wants them to be. The remaining 611 are merely instances of what it looks like to love God and to love others. Jesus turned the number 613 into two.

There are only two commandments: Love God. Love others. If you love God and love others, you do all God wants of you. No wonder people flocked to Jesus: he found the relational core to the will of God when he reduced the laws to the Jesus Creed. (Pages 51–52, OL)

> The first word that should come to mind when we hear Jesus say "kingdom" is the word *love*. In the Kingdom.Life, the King, the King's land, and the citizens of the King are those who love God and who love others (as they love themselves). When Jesus stands up tall and announces that the kingdom has drawn near, he is saying that a society shaped by love is about to take the dance floor and show us how to dance. (Page 53, OL)
>
> When we live in love, we live in the kingdom society Jesus came to create.
>
> Now we have another line in our understanding of how Jesus understood the Christian life.
>
> *A Christian is one who follows Jesus by devoting her or his One.Life to the kingdom of God, fired by Jesus' own imagination, and to a life of loving God and loving others.* (Page 54, OL)

Reflection questions on the reading

1. After having said the Jesus Creed so many times in this study, what did you think when learning more about the context of this saying of Jesus?

2. Explain how Jesus transformed the understanding and interpretation of the Torah in his time.

3. What is the number-one value that shapes the kingdom?

BIBLE STUDY

Jesus Sizzles the Teachers of the Law and Pharisees (Matthew 23)

> Two things resulted from this "follow Torah by adding rules" approach. The first one is that Jesus thought this completely misunderstood how to do Torah. The second, which follows from the first one, is that an increasing number of ordinary folks were cut off from their faith. The leaders had "othered" the ordinary, they had marginalized the common person, and Jesus didn't like it because he thought they were misunderstanding what the Torah was all about. Hence the vehemence of his words. (Page 51, OL)

Read Matthew 23:1–12.

1. Why does Jesus distinguish between doing what the teachers of the law and Pharisees *say* and doing what they *do*?

2. How does Jesus challenge the religious power hierarchy of his day?

Read Matthew 23:13–33.

3. List the seven "woes" Jesus speaks to the teachers of the law and the Pharisees.

4. What does Jesus call them in verse 33?

PRAYER

Meet up with someone in your group so the two of you can pray for each other together. Your group relationships are important as a whole, but so are the individual relationships within the group. Try to express your love for your neighbor as you pray for one another.

As you conclude your prayer time, pray the Lord's Prayer:

> *Our Father in heaven, hallowed be your name, your kingdom come, your will be done, on earth as it is in heaven. Give us today our daily bread. And forgive us our debts, as we also have forgiven our debtors. And lead us not into temptation, but deliver us from the evil one, for yours is the kingdom and the power and the glory forever. Amen. (Matthew 6:9–13)*

ACTION

By the way, if you substitute the specially designed "rulings" in your community of faith into the sayings of Jesus . . . and then declare the remix to your community, you'll probably discover how Jesus was treated by the experts of his day. (Page 51, OL)

Just as the Jews of Jesus' time had the 613 commands, your religious community today may have a long list of rules. List some of them here.

Now cross them all out and write in red on top of them: "Love God and Love People."

REFLECTION

Do you feel more like you are one of the Pharisees or one of the people struggling under the burdens of the rules from religious leaders? What do you think Jesus would say to you today about where you find yourself in this equation?

▪ GROUP DISCUSSION ▪

When your group meeting begins, say the Jesus Creed together:

Hear, O Israel, the Lord our God, the Lord is one. Love the Lord your God with all your heart, with all your soul, with all your mind, and with all your strength. The second is this: love your neighbor as yourself. There is no commandment greater than these.

The following questions are based on the personal study you already have completed. Monitor how much time your group has for discussion and answer as many of these questions together as you can.

READING

- Discuss this line from the reading: "Jesus was deconstructive and constructive." How did the reading demonstrate this?

- How do you think you could be both deconstructive and constructive in approaching your religious environment today?

BIBLE STUDY

- What did you think of Jesus' strong language?

- What was your favorite phrase Jesus used in the Bible study?

- Do you lean toward legalism or permissiveness in your religious practice?

How does Jesus' command to love affect you?

PRAYER

Share about your meeting with another group member to pray.

ACTION

Make a piece of artwork with part or all of the Jesus Creed on it that you can hang somewhere in your house. Use it to remind yourself that the core of all God's commands in the Bible is love. This can be as simple as drawing it on a piece of paper or it can be more complicated. The group leader or another volunteer from the group can bring art supplies: paper, canvas, pottery, poster board, woodburning tools, markers, washi tape, paints and brushes, calligraphy pens, spray paint, or even nails and string and hammers and boards for string art . . . whatever your group wants to do! If the project will take a long time, start it at the beginning of the meeting so everyone can work on their pieces while you have your discussion.

REFLECTION

Share some of the religious rules you came up with in your lists. Which ones are about loving God or loving others?

GROUP PRAYER

Break up into pairs to pray for each other—different partners than you met with earlier in the week.

As your group meeting ends, pray the Lord's Prayer together:

> *Our Father in heaven, hallowed be your name, your kingdom come, your will be done, on earth as it is in heaven. Give us today our daily bread. And forgive us our debts, as we also have forgiven our debtors. And lead us not into temptation, but deliver us from the evil one, for yours is the kingdom and the power and the glory forever. Amen. (Matthew 6:9–13)*

REST

How does it make you feel to think about all religious rules being boiled down to simply "love God and love people"? Allow this freedom and clarity to bring you a sense of rest.

15

LESSON 15

JUSTICE LIFE

Learning intent: Disciples will see Jesus' clear focus on justice in his ministry.
Spiritual formation intent: Disciples will recognize that following Jesus includes sharing his passion for justice.

■ PERSONAL STUDY ■

READING

As you begin your discipleship time today, say the Jesus Creed out loud:

Hear, O Israel, the Lord our God, the Lord is one. Love the Lord your God with all your heart, with all your soul, with all your mind, and with all your strength. The second is this: love your neighbor as yourself. There is no commandment greater than these.

Recently Kris and I were in Stellenbosch, South Africa. On our way to the airport we drove alongside Khayaletsha, an informal settlement for both South Africans and immigrants. . . . Twenty-five miles of little more than corrugated steel shacks with flimsy electric wires strung to each shack—maybe a mile or two wide. In this settlement there are 1.2 million desperately poor people. When Jesus said, "blessed are the poor," was he thinking of such places and such people? Do you think they had anything to do with why Jesus came?

I do.

Care for the poor has everything to do with being a follower of Jesus and how we understand the Christian life.

American Christians have wobbled, are wobbling, and will wobble. They can worship the God of all creation and institutionalize slavery. American Christians can preach a gospel for all and deny women a right to vote. American Christians can follow a Jesus who was poor and themselves chase the dream of opulence. American Christians can write world history textbooks for public schools and ignore major people groups and cultures like Native Americans. . . . American Christians can affirm "justice for all" and commit injustices in their homes and neighborhoods and churches and society.

Young Christians—and I say "Christians" because the people I'm talking about grew up in a church—find this wobbling justice unacceptable . . . Some know the needs are great and issues are serious, so they are both ramping up their commitment to what Jesus says about justice and walking away from the faith.

I have to admit that, however much I embrace a broken church as the only kind of church we will see this side of the full kingdom of God, the faith they are walking away from may not deserve their presence, because Jesus is not there. Having a wobbly commitment to justice is not the way of Jesus.

Jesus was a Galilean prophet. The top two lines on every prophet's job description look like this:

Speak openly and clearly about what God is for.
Speak openly and clearly about what God is against.
The third and fourth lines look like this:
I [God] am with you.
Have courage. (But you may have to duck or die.)

Often you can learn what a person is *for* by listening to what they are *against.* I'll give you what Jesus was against, and you can infer what he was for:
Jesus spoke against authorities who ignored oppression.
He spoke against the tax collectors who ripped people off.
He spoke against his disciples when they ignored the children.

Once you determine what Jesus was against in these lines, you can determine two things: what he was *for* and *why Jesus came to earth.* There's nothing wobbly about Jesus when it comes to what he is for and why he came—he's for proper uses of power, for justice, for the value of everyone. He knew God was with him, and he had courage.

The belief . . . that the kingdom has been reduced to an inner experience, messes up Christians every day. Many think Jesus came to earth so you and I can have a special kind of spiritual experience and then go merrily along, as long as we pray and read our Bibles and develop intimacy with the unseen God but ignore the others-oriented life of justice and love and peace that Jesus embodied. When I hear Christians describe the Christian life as little more than soul development and personal intimacy with God, and I do hear this often, I have to wonder if Christians even really read their Bibles. I mean really read them so that the utter realities of Jesus are seen for what they are. (Pages 58–60, OL)

There are [people] who think Jesus means business when he says, "Follow me." And they know that followers of Jesus (really do) follow Jesus. They also know if you don't follow Jesus, you really aren't a follower of Jesus. . . . Any vision of Jesus that doesn't land squarely on the word *kingdom* isn't the vision of Jesus, and the word *justice* is inside the word *kingdom*. (Page 65, OL)

Why did he come? . . .

Jesus came to bring justice by building the kingdom society on earth beginning right now with you and with me. (Page 67, OL)

Jesus envisions a society marked so deeply by justice that, instead of using power to rule over others, his kingdom people will use their power to *serve one another in a life of sacrifice*. Jesus died, in part, to make that kind of kingdom community spring to life.

BUT YOU MUST BE SAYING . . .

Jesus is either an idealist or his followers have screwed it up completely. The former is true because Jesus was a dreamer and the Dream Awakener. The second statement is also true. It is an embarrassment to look at how so many (who call themselves) followers of Jesus don't follow Jesus. . . . Instead of living the long defeat of the cross, we live for the constant triumph.

I find many today are asking: Do I want to follow the dream Jesus gave us? . . .

To follow Jesus means to follow Jesus into a society where justice rules, where love shapes everything. To follow Jesus means to take up his dream and work for it.

We can now add another clause to our question's answer:

A Christian is one who follows Jesus by devoting her or his One.Life to the kingdom of God, fired by Jesus' own imagination, to a life of loving God and loving others, and to a society shaped by justice, especially for those who have been marginalized. (Pages 69–70, OL)

Reflection questions on the reading

1. Which part of the reading most stood out to you? Why?

2. What do you think is the connection between Christianity and justice?

3. What does justice for the marginalized involve?

BIBLE STUDY

Who Is in the Kingdom? (Luke 6)

People love the Beatitudes of Jesus, but I fear they read them wrong. The Beatitudes are not Jesus' list of virtues but Jesus' revolutionary announcement that those who thought they were in the kingdom . . . were not, and those who thought they were not in the kingdom really were. Imagine what it would have been like for a poor Galilean to hear these words, and then imagine what it would have been like to be a rich Galilean and hear these words. . . .

These words are in your Bible and in mine. This is no list of moral virtues, but a revolutionary way of revealing who is on the Lord's side and who is not. Who is living the Kingdom.Life to the full and who is not. Who is in the kingdom and who is not. Who is living the Dream behind all dreams and who is not. (Pages 65–66, OL)

Read Luke 6:7–26.

1. What tangible evidence does Jesus give of his power and mission in the opening verses?

2. Who does Jesus say will be blessed?

3. To whom does Jesus predict woe?

4. Which descriptions apply to you? In which category do you find yourself?

5. **Bonus study:** If you want to continue your Bible study, read Matthew chapters 5 through 7 and compare the teachings of Jesus there to his teachings in Luke chapter 6. Which appear in both accounts? Which are the same? Which are different? Which ones are unique to one gospel but not the other?

PRAYER

Look at yourself in the mirror. Ask God to help you see in yourself the ways you have participated in injustice. How have you propped up or benefitted from power structures or social systems that oppress people? Ask God to give you Jesus' prophetic passion to bring kingdom justice, preaching good news to poor people and liberation to oppressed people.

As you conclude your prayer time, pray the Lord's Prayer:

> *Our Father in heaven, hallowed be your name, your kingdom come, your will be done, on earth as it is in heaven. Give us today our daily bread. And forgive us our debts, as we also have forgiven our debtors. And lead us not into temptation, but deliver us from the evil one, for yours is the kingdom and the power and the glory forever. Amen. (Matthew 6:9–13)*

ACTION

In his book *A Fellowship of Differents*, Scot quotes from Christena Cleveland's book *Disunity in Christ*. Dr. Cleveland wrote an article on the difference between equality and equity, which is an important concept in working toward justice. Read her article that examines one of Jesus' parables and discusses privilege and oppression in justice: http://www.christenacleveland.com/blog/2016/12/new-series-how-to-be-last-a-practical-theology-for-privileged-people

REFLECTION

How does Dr. Cleveland's article make you feel? What are your initial reactions? What do you think about her distinction between equality and equity? How can you find your place in working for God's kingdom justice?

▪ GROUP DISCUSSION ▪

When your group meeting begins, say the Jesus Creed together:

Hear, O Israel, the Lord our God, the Lord is one. Love the Lord your God with all your heart, with all your soul, with all your mind, and with all your strength. The second is this: love your neighbor as yourself. There is no commandment greater than these.

The following questions are based on the personal study you already have completed. Monitor how much time your group has for discussion and answer as many of these questions together as you can.

READING

- What do you think about justice?

- Is there a difference between God's justice and worldly justice?

- What does justice look like in the mission of Jesus?

BIBLE STUDY

- Where do you see yourself in Jesus' sermon?

- How does the list of blessings give you hope?

- How does the list of woes help you examine yourself?

PRAYER

What did you think about looking at yourself while praying this week? What did God help you see in yourself?

ACTION

1. The group facilitator should look up Amos 2:6b–7a (the last half of verse 6 and the first half of verse 7). Copy it into a word processing document and make the words large. Print it out and cut out each individual word. Mix them up. Ask the group to try to put the words in order to make a coherent verse.
2. Look up a video of a "privilege walk" online. This is an exercise that invites people to step forward based on their various privileged characteristics to show the inherent benefits people hold as they go through life. Watch together as a group. Consider trying this with your group to help each of you understand your own privilege. Discuss with each other how you can use your privilege and status to serve others in your work for justice and equity.

REFLECTION

Discuss your reactions to the Christena Cleveland article. Do responses differ in the group based on whether the person speaking is part of a privileged group versus part of a marginalized or oppressed group? How do group members view their own privilege?

GROUP PRAYER

Let each group member pray for a justice issue that concerns them. The person sitting next to them can then add a prayer for that person's concern, and then pray for their own justice concern. This can continue around the circle.

As your group meeting ends, pray the Lord's Prayer together:

Our Father in heaven, hallowed be your name, your kingdom come, your will be done, on earth as it is in heaven. Give us today our daily bread. And forgive us our debts, as we also have forgiven our debtors. And lead us not into temptation, but deliver us from the evil one, for yours is the kingdom and the power and the glory forever. Amen. (Matthew 6:9–13)

REST

If you need justice—if you have been oppressed, abused, or victimized in any way—find rest in Jesus' deep care for you and his work for freedom and justice.

If you discovered injustice in yourself, find rest in the transforming power of the Holy Spirit to make you like Jesus, laying down power instead of lording authority over other people.

16

LESSON 16

WISDOM LIFE

> **Learning intent:** Disciples will learn ways that Jesus practiced wisdom.
>
> **Spiritual formation intent:** Disciples will try out historical spiritual practices and disciplines that can bring the wisdom of the church mothers and fathers into their lives.

▪ PERSONAL STUDY ▪

READING

As you begin your discipleship time today, say the Jesus Creed out loud:

Hear, O Israel, the Lord our God, the Lord is one. Love the Lord your God with all your heart, with all your soul, with all your mind, and with all your strength. The second is this: love your neighbor as yourself. There is no commandment greater than these.

> Just before David died he announced that his son Solomon would be the next king. Very early in Solomon's career God asked Solomon a question. . . ."I will give you whatever you want, so what do you want?" . . .
>
> Solomon, who can have anything he wants, asks for wisdom. (Page 85, OL)
>
> Tragically, what Solomon *asked* for and how he *acted* were poles part. Solomon brilliantly asked for wisdom, but Solomon acted like a fool as he aged. Solomon's dream became unsustainable and it unraveled. . . .
>
> It's easier to ask for wisdom than to live it. . . .
>
> . . . there are so many examples of those who, like Solomon, begin well and seem to be going in the right direction, but whose moral life comes undone . . .

We need to slow down in life and let wisdom have its way with us. If we want our big dreams to become sustainable, and if we want to end our lives well, we will need to listen to the wise. (Page 86, OL)

> Wisdom is about
> the reverence
> of receiving
> the wisdom of the wise.

Solomon was the fool because he stopped receiving the wisdom of God. James [writer of the book of James] was wise because he received the wisdom of the Wise One. That's the wise posture of a follower of Jesus. Wise people sound like their mentors. (Page 87, OL)

Jesus was the Wise One, and so what I'd like to do is suggest elements in Jesus' own life and teachings that can help us orient our lives toward wisdom . . .

#1: ORIENT EACH DAY TOWARD GOD.

Jesus grew up listening to a famous, famous line from Solomon: "The fear of the Lord is the beginning of wisdom" (Proverbs 9:10). The word *fear* does not suggest cowering or cringing or buckling or breaking down . . . No, this fear means "awe." . . . To fear God is to begin and end your day, and every moment between, with a consciousness of living with and before God.

#2: ASK THE "GOOD QUESTION" ALL DAY LONG UNTIL IT BECOMES HABIT.

. . . A wise person stops, thinks, ponders, and probes into her conscience and then asks: "Is this the wise thing to do?" Jesus, who was wisdom itself, did what was good and right and kind and just and holy and loving. . . . If we ask ourselves the right question, we will do what is good. (Page 89, OL)

#3: THE DAILY LEADS TO THE DREAM.

Jesus' dream was the Kingdom.Life, and his dream was for the whole world. That's a big dream.

How did he go about his big kingdom dream? Did he march off to Jerusalem and say, "I want this throne!" Did he get in a big boat and head off to Rome and say to Caesar, "There is no Caesar but me!" No. . . . Jesus' approach, wisely, was to take one step at a time, and it began in Nazareth and shifted over to the Sea of Galilee a few miles and then he gathered disciples. He helped and he healed; he taught and he mentored; he listened and he observed; he did kingdom living daily. . . .

It works both ways:

Focus on the daily instead of the dream, but . . .

Let the dream shape what you do daily. (Page 90, OL)

#4: WHAT YOU WANT TO DO OVER THERE BEGINS HERE.

What Jesus really wanted was to rule as God's Messiah on the throne. The Thief understood this and that is why he offered Jesus the temple and the world in the temptations of Jesus right after his baptism. Jesus' dream meant a throne in Jerusalem and then one in Rome. But observe where Jesus began . . .

Jesus started a revolution by gathering around him his personal family and local friends, and it grew from the small to the big. The wise thing to do is begin now with where you are and let that dream shape everyday living. (Pages 90–91, OL)

#5: EVERYDAY PEOPLE ARE TO BE EVERYDAY NEIGHBORS.

Everyday people became everyday neighbors to Jesus, because he loved every person he met. It is so easy to pass by those in our immediate circle (family, friends, neighbors) in order to show compassion to those in Africa or Southeast Asia or the inner city. But Jesus treated everyone as a neighbor. The wise thing is to see every person as someone loved by God, and that changes everyday people into your everyday neighbors. (Pages 91–92, OL)

#6: DISCOVER WHO YOU ARE BY LOVING OTHERS.

. . . by loving others we find ourselves, by giving ourselves to others we receive soul-shaping life, and by serving others we find ourselves at our deepest core. But if we think "me, me, me," we diminish ourselves . . . [Jesus] lived *for* others and it was living *for* others that brought Kingdom. Life. In relating to others we find ourselves; in hiding ourselves from others, we lose ourselves. (Pages 92–93, OL)

#7 ENEMIES CAN BE LOVED EASIER THAN CONQUERED.

Jesus extended love even to his enemies . . . If God loves all, so should God's followers. Even enemies. . . .

The way to make friends of your enemies is to love them and to pray for them. The way to keep them your enemies is to avoid learning their names and to avoid getting to know them. But if we pray for them, we will transform them from enemies into friends. Jesus did the wise thing when he told his followers to love their enemies and sacrifice the temporary, unsustainable thrill of hatred on the altar of enemy-love. (Pages 93–94, OL)

One more time, our question:

According to Jesus, what is a Christian?

A Christian is one who follows Jesus by devoting her or his One.Life to the kingdom of God, fired by Jesus' own imagination, to a life of loving God and loving others, and to a society shaped by justice, especially for those who have been marginalized, to peace, and to a life devoted to acquiring wisdom. (Page 95, OL)

Reflection questions on the reading

1. Which of the seven ideas about wisdom from Jesus' life is the easiest for you to practice? Why?

2. Which is the hardest? Why?

3. What does Jesus' example of pursuing his dream and mission inspire you to do as you pursue your own God-given dreams?

4. Think of a well-known leader or a leader you know whose life fell apart. What role do you think wisdom played or didn't play in their life?

BIBLE STUDY

Get Wisdom (Proverbs 4)

Read Proverbs 4.

1. Copy down all the references to wisdom.

2. What examples of good and bad decisions are given?

3. Wisdom is personified as a woman in this poem. Describe her.

PRAYER

The prayers of the historical and global church can bring wisdom into our lives. Try praying liturgical prayers. You can look up the daily prayers:

For Anglicans: https://universalis.com/
For Catholics: https://www.pbs.org.uk/the-bcp/daily-office-online

Choose a time of day when you are praying (morning or evening for the Anglican prayers, multiple times in the day for the Catholic prayers) and click on the corresponding link. You'll find a long set of mostly-Scripture based prayers and readings. Read them out loud and go through the whole set. If you enjoy it, consider choosing a day and praying all the set prayers at the set times.

ACTION

Let me urge you to find someone who is wise, someone who is loving, someone who is just, someone who is peaceful, and ask them if you can regularly spend time with them. Tell them they don't need to pull out a "lesson" each day or prepare anything. Ask them if you can spend time with them and do life with them once a week or once a month, so you can hear their wisdom and absorb it.

Now the hard part. I'm going to ask you not only to find a mentor and listen to a mentor, but to do everything you can to do what the mentor advises you to do. The wise are those who are receptively reverent enough toward the wise that they listen and do what the wise advise. (Page 88, OL)

▨ Think of several people who fit these criteria. Write their names below. Contact one of them today to ask if they will mentor you.

Determine to ask the good question all day long one day: *"Is this the wise thing to do?"* Choose a day this week, and every time you face a decision, ask yourself that question.

REFLECTION

What did you think about the experience of praying set prayers, especially if this was your first time? Describe your thoughts, reflections, and feelings. What did you like or dislike about it? Is this a spiritual practice you would like to continue? Why or why not?

▪ GROUP DISCUSSION ▪

When your group meeting begins, say the Jesus Creed together:

Hear, O Israel, the Lord our God, the Lord is one. Love the Lord your God with all your heart, with all your soul, with all your mind, and with all your strength. The second is this: love your neighbor as yourself. There is no commandment greater than these.

The following questions are based on the personal study you already have completed. Monitor how much time your group has for discussion and answer as many of these questions together as you can.

READING

▪ Can you think of other examples from Jesus' life when he showed wisdom?

▪ As you have been doing this workbook, have you noticed yourself growing in love for your neighbors?

▪ Who are the enemies you have a hard time loving?

BIBLE STUDY

▪ Has someone in your life urged you to get wisdom like the Proverbs writers urges the son?

▪ Which verse about wisdom was your favorite?

PRAYER/REFLECTION

Discuss your experiences with liturgical prayer. Which prayers did you use? Which time of day did you pray? What did you like and dislike? How did you feel about praying out loud alone?

ACTION

The orthodox statements of the historical church can bring wisdom into our lives. Look up the Nicene Creed together and let each group member copy it out by hand. When you are all done, say it out loud together.

GROUP PRAYER

Sing your group prayer today. The doxology is a short song written several hundred years ago. It begins, "Praise God from whom all blessings flow." If you don't know it, look up an audio or video recording. Sing it together as a group.

As your group meeting ends, pray the Lord's Prayer together:

> *Our Father in heaven, hallowed be your name, your kingdom come, your will be done, on earth as it is in heaven. Give us today our daily bread. And forgive us our debts, as we also have forgiven our debtors. And lead us not into temptation, but deliver us from the evil one, for yours is the kingdom and the power and the glory forever. Amen. (Matthew 6:9–13)*

REST

Find recordings of liturgical prayers being read, for example, the Orthodox Shehimo prayers. Listen to them as you rest.

17

LESSON 17

VOCATION LIFE

Learning intent: Disciples will learn that all jobs matter in the kingdom of God. There are no unimportant vocations.

Spiritual formation intent: Disciples will look at principles that can help them change the way they view their jobs and grow in seeing their vocations as opportunities to live as followers of Jesus.

▪ PERSONAL STUDY ▪

READING

As you begin your discipleship time today, say the Jesus Creed out loud:

Hear, O Israel, the Lord our God, the Lord is one. Love the Lord your God with all your heart, with all your soul, with all your mind, and with all your strength. The second is this: love your neighbor as yourself. There is no commandment greater than these.

I know people who are lawyers and people who drive big machines and who are school teachers and who are coaches and who sell insurance and who are accountants and who are science research professors and who are dentists and who are pastors and who are missionaries. What each of these people does matters. I kept thinking about this word *matters*. I'm unconvinced that some jobs—the so-called "spiritual" ones—are valuable while others are "secular" and therefore not as valuable. . . .

I believe there is a way of making everything you do matter, and it comes by attending once again to the kingdom dream of Jesus. But recent conclusions reveal that many are struggling to discover a career that matters. Perhaps the search for the elusive dream-career that matters is, well, unexamined, and perhaps this unexamined career is what is causing all the confusion in the above conclusions. So I want to make a claim for you to consider:

The unexamined vocation leads to what does not "matter."

BUT

The examined vocation will "matter."

Perhaps the reason so many today flounder from one job to another is because instead of examining what they do in light of the kingdom, they fail to realize that what they are doing really does matter. (Unless they are paid to be professional spammers, which can't be kingdom work.) It is time to reconsider what we do in light of the kingdom dream of Jesus, and I believe his kingdom vision can turn what we do into something that matters and can give our One.Life purpose.

Remember your dreams are glimpses of the Jesus kingdom dream. Your vocation, which in so many ways is unique to you, can genuinely matter if you keep your eyes on the kingdom of God as your guiding North Star. Teaching matters when you treat your students as humans whom you love and whom you are helping. Coaching soccer matters when you connect kids to the kingdom. Growing vegetables becomes kingdom work when we enjoy God's green world as a gift from him. Collecting taxes becomes kingdom work when you treat each person as someone who is made in the image (the *Eikon* in Greek) of God and as a citizen instead of as a suspect. Jobs become vocations and begin to matter when we connect what we do to God's kingdom vision for this world. Sure, there's scut work involved—like learning English grammar well enough to write clean sentences and reading great writers who can show you how good prose works. Like hours in the weight room and running sprints so you can become good enough to compete at high levels and learn the game of soccer so you can pass it on. Like long hours in the office in your early career to learn the ropes and master the job. Like hours with small children when we are challenged to make some mind-numbing routines into habits of the heart and kingdom.

It is easy to see missional work in the slums of India as something that matters. Perhaps the desire to do something that matters is why so many of us get involved in missional work like that. But most of us don't have a vocation like that, and that means most of us do lots of scut work as a matter of routine. We have to believe that the mundane matters to God, and the way to make the mundane matter is to baptize what we do in the kingdom vision of Jesus.

. . . Because God is at work in whatever we do, we need to see we are doing much more than making money. (Pages 145–48, OL)

> Jesus' dream involved a radical detachment from possessions:
> But seek first his kingdom
> and his righteousness
> And all these things [clothing, food, shelter]
> will be given to you as well.
>
> *Matthew 6:33*

It involved a willingness to contribute to the needs of others and virtually to renounce a life soaked in making money:

> Sell your possessions and give to the poor.
>
> *Luke 12:33*

While many in the history of the Church gave up everything they owned in order to serve others, and I think of St. Basil and St. Francis of Assisi, the rest of us are challenged to cut back and to tone it down so we can take from our abundance and provide for those who are in need.

When the Lord of the Christian is a poor man, the wealth of his followers is brought into embarrassing clarity. When the kingdom dream of Jesus shapes our vocations, it turns us from folks who strive for wealth into folks whose vocations are used for others. (Page 149, OL)

If you keep your eye on the kingdom of God, if you keep in mind that deeply personal nature of all you do, then you can pursue that place where your deepest gladness and the world's deepest needs meet, and in that place your life will speak. You are asked merely to discern the intersection of what God is doing—kingdom of God—and what you are asked to do in what God's doing. (Pages 153–54, OL)

Let me ask you again about what matters. Too many think what matters is something huge and splashy and earth-shattering and world-reversing and far-off-land-saving. For many what matters must take place in a church or in a parachurch organization. But that's not true. What really matters is that you do what God made you to do, that you live that piece of God's dream that God gave to you. (Page 156, OL)

Reflection questions on the reading

1. What are some of the ideas from the reading about what makes a vocation "matter"?

2. How can we separate the value of a vocation from how much money it makes?

3. What is the "scut work" in your vocation?

BIBLE STUDY

Workin' It

Paul gave various instructions about work to the Christians who received his letters.

Read Colossians 3:23–24.

1. With what attitude did Paul tell people to approach their work?

2. What principle in these verses can help you see your work as something that matters?

Read 2 Thessalonians 3:6–12.

3. What does Paul say about his own work ethic?

4. How does he instruct the Thessalonians to approach work?

Read 1 Timothy 5:3–8.

5. What instructions does Paul give about providing for widows?

6. How does this affect the way you look at providing financially for others as giving meaning to your work, regardless of your job?

PRAYER

Are you unemployed or underemployed? Are you frustrated in your job? Are you considering a career change? Pray about your work struggles. Ask God to provide for you and to enable you to provide for others.

As you conclude your prayer time, pray the Lord's Prayer:

Our Father in heaven, hallowed be your name, your kingdom come, your will be done, on earth as it is in heaven. Give us today our daily bread. And forgive us our debts, as we also have forgiven our debtors. And lead us not into temptation, but deliver us from the evil one, for yours is the kingdom and the power and the glory forever. Amen. (Matthew 6:9–13)

ACTION

Watch the *Doctor Who* episode "Rosa" (Series 11, episode 3). It's a standalone episode that makes sense even if you don't know the series.

- What is Rosa Parks's job? How does she view her paid work? How does she view her outside-work-hours community organizing vocation? How does she take faithful daily steps toward her dream? What prepares her for her life-changing moment?

REFLECTION

- What is your dream vocation? If money weren't the limiting factor, what kind of work would you love to do? Write a job description for the ideal work for you. How do you want to live out kingdom life in your vocation?

■ GROUP DISCUSSION ■

When your group meeting begins, say the Jesus Creed together:

Hear, O Israel, the Lord our God, the Lord is one. Love the Lord your God with all your heart, with all your soul, with all your mind, and with all your strength. The second is this: love your neighbor as yourself. There is no commandment greater than these.

The following questions are based on the personal study you already have completed. Monitor how much time your group has for discussion and answer as many of these questions together as you can.

READING

- Share about your jobs with each other, either current jobs or positions you've worked in the past.

- What have you learned about vocation in your life?

- How can you see your work or study or occupation right now as something that matters?

- How can you transform your occupation into something that matters in the kingdom of God?

BIBLE STUDY

- What biblical principles did you learn about work?

- In what ways did your study challenge you to rethink your approach to work?

PRAYER

- What are your concerns or frustrations about employment that you prayed about?

ACTION

Is there anyone in your group who needs help finding a job or changing jobs? Anyone who needs encouragement to stick with what they're doing and find meaning in it? Encourage each other to follow Jesus in the way you live your vocational life. If you can help each other in any practical ways, arrange to do this. Networking, editing résumés, recommending them for a job, following up and providing accountability, helping them get interview or work clothes, providing child-care so they can get to work, sorting out transportation issues . . .

REFLECTION

For those who are willing, read your dream vocation description to the rest of the group.

GROUP PRAYER

Pray Scripture for each other. The group facilitator can print out Bible verses about work with blanks where group members can insert each other's names as they pray for each other. Here are some examples:

God, help _____ give generously to others and bless them in all their work
    and in everything they put their hand to (from Deuteronomy 15:10).
God, please help _____ never get tired of doing good (2 Thessalonians 3:13).
God, help _____ work with all their heart, as working for you, knowing they
    will receive an inheritance from you (from Colossians 3:23).

As your group meeting ends, pray the Lord's Prayer together:

Our Father in heaven, hallowed be your name, your kingdom come, your will be done, on earth as it is in heaven. Give us today our daily bread. And forgive us our debts, as we also have forgiven our debtors. And lead us not into temptation, but deliver us from the evil one, for yours is the kingdom and the power and the glory forever. Amen. (Matthew 6:9–13)

REST

As you look at your work life, think about how you are making time for Sabbath rest. Are you taking regular pauses from work to devote time and energy to rest and worship?

There are seasons of life when that just seems impossible—perhaps you come home from a job to young children who need care, or perhaps you are home with children all day. Maybe you work two or three jobs or one really demanding job. Maybe your commute is exhausting or your schedule is unpredictable. There are times when trying to find time to rest feels like just one more burden. Share this with your small group. Ask them to help you in practical ways so that you can rest.

18

LESSON 18

ETERNITY LIFE

> **Learning intent:** Disciples will learn Jesus' views on life after death (and death after death).
> **Spiritual formation intent:** Disciples will work to align their views and expectations of future life with Jesus'.

■ PERSONAL STUDY ■

READING

As you begin your discipleship time today, say the Jesus Creed out loud:

Hear, O Israel, the Lord our God, the Lord is one. Love the Lord your God with all your heart, with all your soul, with all your mind, and with all your strength. The second is this: love your neighbor as yourself. There is no commandment greater than these.

Pre-reading questions:

1. What do you think happens to people after they die?

2. What do you think about heaven and hell?

I believe in heaven. I believe in heaven because Jesus did, and I hope I believe in heaven *as* Jesus did. I believe in heaven because I believe in justice, in peace, and in love. . . . I believe that what is forever and ever is called the New Heavens and the New Earth, the time and the place where heaven comes down to earth. The New Heavens and the New Earth will be the fullness of flourishing.

But belief in the New Heavens and the New Earth also means I believe in hell. I believe in hell because Jesus did. And I hope I believe in hell *as* Jesus believed in hell. I believe in hell because I believe in justice, in peace, and in love. . . . I don't believe in Dante's hell or in God as the grand torturer. Hell will be the end of flourishing. (Page 159, OL)

[Jesus'] kingdom dream was primarily shaped by a glorious vision of the New Heavens and New Earth, but also by a hell, and the following words make this abundantly clear:

> Do not be afraid of those who kill the body but cannot kill the soul. Rather, be afraid of the One who can destroy both soul and body in **hell**.
>
> *Matthew 10:28*

> If your hand or your foot causes you to stumble, cut it off and throw it away. It is better for you to enter life maimed or crippled than to have two hands or two feet and be thrown into **eternal fire**. And if your eye causes you to stumble, gouge it out and throw it away. It is better for you to enter **life** with one eye than to have two eyes and be thrown into the fire of **hell**.
>
> *Matthew 18:8–9*

Jesus clearly believed *that* there was life after death and he clearly believed in what I want to call "*death after death*" too. In short, Jesus believed that after we die we will meet our Maker and will have to account for whether or not we entered the narrow gate, bore good fruit, acknowledged Jesus publicly, and lived good lives that treated the marginalized with compassion. Jesus believed that our Maker will assign us to one of two places: the life place or the death place. . . . Jesus believed those who didn't follow him, who rejected God's ways and who oppressed others and who waged war against peace and who were unloving and who were foolish in this life would not inherit the kingdom of God and would experience a final endless death after physical death. The scheme would be something like this: we are born, we live, we die, we are raised to judgment, we are judged to death after death. Death after death is awful to consider, but it's extremely foolish not to consider.

Justice, too, demands some kind of belief in final death after death. If there is any theme that drives the future dream of the Bible, it is that on that Day God will finally establish justice. The wonderful song of Mary in Luke 1, called the Magnificat, sings just that note . . . From Moses to the prophets, from Jesus to the end of the book of Revelation, this theme is clear: though injustice may haunt our world right now and though we may experience horrific tragedies in the here and now, the overriding hope is that *someday justice will finally be established*. Our dreams of fairness and our dreams for justice are anchored in this hope that someday God will make all things right.

The kingdom dream of Jesus opens up to us a revelation of God's final future: "may your will be done on earth as it is in heaven." (Pages 161–62, OL)

Jesus prophesied a future kingdom, the dream kingdom come true, and he fashioned it most often as a banquet in a city. The climactic revelation in the book of Revelation concerns a City, the New Jerusalem, and this Eternal City descends from the heavens down to earth so that it is the meeting place of heaven and earth. The single most important implication is this: if the final state is the New Heavens and the New Earth, and the New Heavens and the New Earth are a City on a transformed earth, then the eternal state is the *perfection of life on earth and not an escape from life on earth.* (Page 166, OL)

This New Jerusalem—on earth as it is in heaven—is justice, and it is peace, and it is love, and it is wisdom, and it involves everyone loving God and others with every globule of their being in an endless exploration of the Life God wants of each one of us. The New Jerusalem—on earth as it is in heaven—is the dream kingdom of Jesus in its finality and perfection and glory.

The people of God,
living with God,
and living with one another in perfect shalom and love and justice.

Everyone will be in direct contact with God and the Lamb, whose death brought forgiveness and redemption and liberation . . .

So when Jesus says "kingdom" and he teaches us to dream of that kingdom by praying for that kingdom in the Lord's Prayer, this vision in Revelation 21 is what he has in mind. In the meantime, his followers are seeking to live out that kind of kingdom in the here and now.

. . . the New Heavens and the New Earth is the final state of living with God in God's world as God made it to be. (Page 168, OL)

Reflection questions on the reading

1. What did the reading change in your thinking? How would you answer the pre-reading questions now? (What do you think happens to people after they die? What do you think about heaven and hell?)

2. How do you feel about the idea that justice demands a belief in death after death?

3. What do you see as the differences between the idea of leaving earth for a faraway heaven versus the idea of a New Heaven and New Earth joining together in New Creation?

4. How do the different ideas affect how you live life now?

BIBLE STUDY

The End (Revelation 21)

Jesus' beloved friend and disciple John was the only one of the Twelve who died a natural death at an old age. Before he died, he wrote down his visions along with messages from Jesus for the churches he cared about.

Read Revelation 21.

1. Describe your overall impression as you read this chapter. What did you think? What did you feel?

2. Does this vision sound appealing to you? Why or why not?

3. List some of the physical descriptions John gives of this New Creation.

4. How do you think John felt in receiving this vision and looking forward to seeing it fulfilled?

PRAYER

Try a wordless prayer. Picture this scene that John describes, with all the hopes and possibilities. Make your ideas and feelings and senses open to God. Don't worry about putting your thoughts into words.

As you conclude your prayer time, pray the Lord's Prayer:

Our Father in heaven, hallowed be your name, your kingdom come, your will be done, on earth as it is in heaven. Give us today our daily bread. And forgive us our debts, as we also have forgiven our debtors. And lead us not into temptation, but deliver us from the evil one, for yours is the kingdom and the power and the glory forever. Amen. (Matthew 6:9–13)

ACTION

Listen to the song by Lecrae called "It Is What It Is" and look up and read the lyrics. Notice the line that sums up this section of the workbook: "I got one life so . . ."

REFLECTION

▪ How are you spending your one life living for the eternal kingdom?

▪ GROUP DISCUSSION ▪

When your group meeting begins, say the Jesus Creed together:

Hear, O Israel, the Lord our God, the Lord is one. Love the Lord your God with all your heart, with all your soul, with all your mind, and with all your strength. The second is this: love your neighbor as yourself. There is no commandment greater than these.

The following questions are based on the personal study you already have completed. Monitor how much time your group has for discussion and answer as many of these questions together as you can.

READING

▪ What surprised you the most in the reading? What were new ideas for you?

▪ Review all the lessons in this section. Which reading was your favorite? Why?

BIBLE STUDY

■ Which details did you like the most in the description of New Creation?

■ Try describing to each other what you picture when you think about these scenes.

PRAYER

How did you find the experience of wordless prayer? Did you feel like you could communicate with God without words?

ACTION/PRAYER

Go for a walk as a group, if the weather/location/health of group members allows it. As you walk, have a conversation with each other and bring God into it. For example, someone could say, "Look at the bird building a nest there! God, thank you that Jesus said we have more value than the sparrows, as he reminded us you will provide." Or someone could say, "I am really worried about my aunt's cancer. She's starting radiation next week. God, would you be with her during the procedure? Please heal her." Share the conversation with each other and with God.

REFLECTION

What did you discover as you journaled about how you are spending your one life?

As your group meeting ends, pray the Lord's Prayer together:

> *Our Father in heaven, hallowed be your name, your kingdom come, your will be done, on earth as it is in heaven. Give us today our daily bread. And forgive us our debts, as we also have forgiven our debtors. And lead us not into temptation, but deliver us from the evil one, for yours is the kingdom and the power and the glory forever. Amen. (Matthew 6:9–13)*

REST

If you had no obligations and no responsibilities, what would you do to relax? Try to make that happen for yourself as you rest from your studies.

PART 4

SHOWING THE GOSPEL

My small group was made up of a local Dutch couple, a South African couple, an Armenian refugee, a Jordanian student, a Kenyan mother, and two Indian families, one from northern India and one from southern. We ate dinner together before our study each week, and the Indian families had an unofficial cooking contest going to promote their own region's food and to see who could make the dish that would finally be spicy enough to defeat my husband's taste buds. One evening, I hosted, and I thought a salad bar would be a universally appealing meal and an easy way to feed a crowd. I laid out all the ingredients on my table, and when it was my turn in line, I piled lettuce on my plate and dumped toppings and dressing on it before stirring it around with my fork. Then I watched one of my Indian friends cautiously select a few items for his plate, making distinct little mountains: a stack of olives here, tomatoes there, chopped peppers, and a few spinach leaves for a garnish. When his wife did the same, I realized I had made a huge mistake, and I asked him about it. He was polite and bemused when he explained, "We don't know how to eat this. We don't eat salad in India."

Over our eight years as a church, we've welcomed people from over one hundred nations. Any given Sunday service includes probably twenty-five nationalities. Though we try to be aware and sensitive, cultural missteps are a part of our church life. So much so that our unofficial motto is: "We embrace the awkward at Damascus Road." When Scot's book *A Fellowship of Differents* came out, I snapped it up, hoping it would be the perfect book to solve all my problems of helping to hold our church's diversity together in unity.

But his central metaphor in the book was about salad.

Everything I learned about the Christian life I learned from my church. I will make this a bigger principle: a local church determines what the Christian life looks like for the people in that church. Now I'll make it even bigger still: we all learn the Christian life from how our local church shapes us . . . Churches determine the direction of our discipleship. Which leads to one big question:

What then is the church supposed to be?

I believe for most of us the church is a place we go on Sunday to hear a sermon, or to participate in worship, or to partake in Communion. Some will add Sunday school classes and time together in the fellowship hall. But by and large it is all contained within one or two hours on Sunday morning. After two hours, we go home and "church" is over. No one wants to admit that is what church really is in practice, but it's true! So we ask that question again, only this time we add a second one:

What is the church supposed to be?

and

If the church is what it is supposed to be, what does the Christian life look like?

To answer that question, I want us to explore the image of the salad bowl, which reflects the ways all us "differents"—from different socioeconomic groups, genders, educational and ethnic backgrounds, and life situations—struggle to come together in fellowship as the church God intended.

There are three ways to eat a salad: the American Way, the Weird Way, and the Right Way. The American Way of eating a salad is to fill your bowl with some iceberg lettuce or some spinach leaves, some tomato slices and olives, and maybe some carrots, then smother it with salad dressing—ranch or Thousand Island or Italian or, for special occasions, Caesar. The Weird Way is to separate each item in your salad around on your plate, then eat them as separate items. People who do this often do not even use dressing. As I said, weird.

Now the Right Way to make and eat a salad is to gather all your ingredients—some spinach, kale, chard, arugula, iceberg lettuce (if you must)—and chop them into smaller bits. Then cut up some tomatoes, carrots, onions, red pepper, and purple cabbage. Add some nuts and dried berries, sprinkle some pecorino romano cheese, and finally drizzle over the salad some good olive oil, which somehow brings the taste of each item to its fullest. Surely this is what God intended when he created "mixed salad."

. . . if we want to get the church right, we have to learn to see it as a salad in a bowl, made the Right Way of course. For a good salad is a fellowship of different tastes, all mixed together with the olive oil accentuating the taste of each. The earliest Christian churches were made up of folks from all over the social map, but they formed a fellowship of "different tastes," a mixed salad of the best kind. (Pages 12–15, FOD)

The book had good advice about love and welcoming that helped me better serve my church, but the metaphor continued to bug me. In my first one-week intensive class on campus at Northern, I caught up to Scot during a break.

"Yo, Scot," I said. (I didn't actually say, "Yo, Scot," but that's how he starts stories about students who ask impertinent questions, so even though I probably said, "Hey, Dr. McKnight," I was still impertinent, so I'll tell the story this way about myself.) "Your main analogy in *Fellowship of Differents* doesn't work! How can you talk about the *right way* to eat salad as a metaphor for church life, when some cultures don't even EAT salad?" And I told him about my church and my failed salad bar.

He responded in a matter-of-fact manner that I now know is satisfaction in his hard-worked conclusions and genuinely not caring what other people think about them. "I didn't write the book for your church."

Oh. Well, then.

"I wrote it for American Christians who shop at Whole Foods," he said. "They eat salad, and many of them need more *differents* in their churches." He told me his original title for the book was *Life in the Salad Bowl*.

My friends Judith, from Indonesia, and Willem, from the Netherlands, are married to each other. They shared a message with our church last Sunday using their marriage as an example of the way multicultural relationships can work in the church. Judith said that they prayed when they first got married, "God, we want to honor you in our marriage. There won't be Indonesian culture, there won't be Dutch culture, there will be Jesus culture." They haven't abandoned their own cultures, but rather they have learned from the good things in each other's cultures. She talked about the apostle Paul's friends in Roman house churches who did the same and were also countercultural—as they formed their Jesus culture together, they went against the ways of the Roman culture that was not pleasing God.

I love my fellowship of differents, even when our salad bowl gets uncomfortable.

Whether your church is mostly made of "sames" or mostly made of "differents" (and whether or not you actually eat salad), these next six lessons will help you consider what it can look like to follow King Jesus together with others in the church. *Grace* enables us to say "Yes" to each other, and *Love* teaches us to develop rugged commitments to be with and for each other and to grow into Christlikeness together. Our gathering at the *Table* for the Lord's Supper is our common ground. Growing in *Holiness* together means being both set apart from the world and devoted to God. We wrestle in the salad bowl as we deal with the *Newness* of a new politics in the kingdom of God, and we are *Flourishing* together when we use the gifts the Spirit gives us to serve each other in love.

19

LESSON 19

GRACE

Learning intent: Disciples will see how grace changed Paul's life and led to the inclusion of gentiles in the Story of Jesus.

Spiritual formation intent: Disciples will confront their prejudices and seek God's grace to help them find unity with people they disagree with.

 PERSONAL STUDY

READING

As you begin your discipleship time today, say the Jesus Creed out loud:

Hear, O Israel, the Lord our God, the Lord is one. Love the Lord your God with all your heart, with all your soul, with all your mind, and with all your strength. The second is this: love your neighbor as yourself. There is no commandment greater than these.

> God looks at all of us and says Yes. Do you hear God's grand Yes to you?. . . It's . . . the best news ever, that God looks at you and says, *Yes, I want you in my company.* God's Yes echoes throughout the cosmic expanse and promises, *I will do what it takes to make that happen.* God's Yes to us . . . is the foundation for our learning to say Yes to those who are different from us in the church . . . (Page 29, FOD)
>
> Look around you in all directions, then look farther—to the northern countries and to the southern countries, to the west and to the east. God's Yes in Jesus is for everyone. Because there is so much variety in this world and because we are so invisible to one another, we need to let God's Yes in Christ penetrate so deeply that we embrace all others as the objects of God's Yes.

We need to know that those who are invisible to us are visible to God and, if they listen, that they too can hear God's Yes.

Paul's new vision of God's grand experiment rubbed raw the delicate skin over ethnic privilege. Jews would have to learn that God was saying Yes to gentiles; gentiles—the Greeks and Romans—would have to learn that God was saying Yes to Jews. Males would have to learn God's Yes spoken to women, and women would have to learn God's Yes spoken to men. The economically elite would have to learn that God's Yes included the poor, and the poor would have to learn that God's Yes involved the rich. The morally kosher would have to listen with better ears for God's Yes to the morally nonkosher—the alcoholics, the prostitutes, and the all-too-common thieves.

God's Yes is why the church is God's great mystery in this world, the place where he is doing something altogether radical and new. Sadly, God's Yes is often the first notion rejected by whites about African Americans, by African Americans about Latin Americans, by Latin Americans about women, by women about men, by rich white men about poor minorities. The revolution God creates in the church begins or ends with this first step: either we embrace that God's Yes is for all or we don't. (Page 31, FOD)

Maybe you've not read Paul's story enough to know the details, but Paul once left Jerusalem under orders from Caiaphas, the high priest, to arrest Christians. He was successfully carrying out those orders when God stepped into his life and transformed him. Remarkably, Paul returned to Jerusalem three years later as a defector from his former rabbi's ways and as a convert to Jesus' ways. . . . Paul knew he was in a place called grace.

Grace is the opening word that tumbles out of Paul's mouth.
Grace is more than being lucky to be on God's side.
Grace is God's goodness showered on people who have failed.
Grace is God's love on those who think they are unlovable.
Grace is God knowing what we are designed to be.
Grace is God believing in us when we have given up.
Grace is someone at the end of their rope finding new strength.

But there's more to grace. Grace is both a place and a power.
Grace is God unleashing his transforming power.
Grace realigns and reroutes a life and a community.
Grace is when you turn your worst enemy into your best friend. (Page 38, FOD)

If we were to sum up Paul's life in three words, it would be these: zeal, grace, transformation. Grace turns God-fighters into God-defenders.

Grace turns Jesus-haters into Jesus-lovers.

Grace turns Spirit-resisters into Spirit-listeners.

To do this, grace forgives; grace heals; grace transforms; grace ennobles; grace empowers. Grace makes people in the salad bowl comfortable with another. Only grace can do that. But grace can do that.

Paul doesn't call the place of grace or the church a "salad bowl." Instead he calls it being "in Christ." . . . To be in Christ means we live in him, we die in him, and we are raised in him. To be in Christ means to be joined to others who are in Christ. . . . To be in Christ means one kind of grace piled on top of another. Grace places us in the salad bowl, gives us an assignment in the salad bowl, and gives us the courage and power to live with others in the salad bowl. (Pages 39–40, FOD)

. . . grace does not begin with God's anger or wrath. No, God's grace begins on the Yes-note of love; grace begins with his unconquerable love for us. He gives us a place "in Christ," and then God's grace empowers us to thrive "in Christ." Grace invades our world to transform us until we are fully outfitted for eternal life. Grace is God's loving, new creation power at work in us. (Page 44, FOD)

Reflection questions on the reading

1. How have you been received by Christians in churches or other Christian gatherings? How have you experienced God's Yes through God's people? If you have experienced rejection from Christians instead of welcome, write about that.

2. How have you heard "grace" used or defined by Christians before?

3. Based on this reading, how would you explain grace?

BIBLE STUDY

Paul Finds Grace (Acts 26 and Ephesians 3)

Read Acts 26:1–23.

1. What is the situation here? Why is Paul telling his story?

2. How did God intervene in Paul's life?

3. What did Paul do in response to Jesus' message to him?

Read Ephesians 3:1–8.

1. How did Paul become a servant of the gospel?

2. Why did God give Paul this gift of grace?

PRAYER

What role has God given you to play in carrying the gospel to all people everywhere? What is the grace God has given you? What are your gifts? What is your mission? Ask God these questions and any others that come to mind. Make time to stay quiet and listen to what God might reveal to you.

As you conclude your prayer time, pray the Lord's Prayer:

> *Our Father in heaven, hallowed be your name, your kingdom come, your will be done, on earth as it is in heaven. Give us today our daily bread. And forgive us our debts, as we also have forgiven our debtors. And lead us not into temptation, but deliver us from the evil one, for yours is the kingdom and the power and the glory forever. Amen. (Matthew 6:9–13)*

ACTION

Think about an issue that's important to you in politics, religion, or social science. Search online for a personal essay or op-ed from a person who holds the opposite view from you. Try not to find a hot-headed or extreme article that would be easy to dismiss, but rather look for a thoughtful piece that includes personal stories and experiences. Read it with a goal of empathizing with the writer. Look for anything you have in common. Approach it with the eyes of grace.

REFLECTION

Grace helps us repeat God's Yes to others. Grace helps make church *God's space for Yes.* When the reading talked about people of different ethnicities, social strata, and genders, what or who came to your mind? If you're honest with yourself, are there people (individuals or groups) with whom you struggle to find unity?

- Who are the *differents* you struggle to love? Why? What could God's grace make possible for you in relating with them?

■ GROUP DISCUSSION ■

When your group meeting begins, say the Jesus Creed together:

Hear, O Israel, the Lord our God, the Lord is one. Love the Lord your God with all your heart, with all your soul, with all your mind, and with all your strength. The second is this: love your neighbor as yourself. There is no commandment greater than these.

The following questions are based on the personal study you already have completed. Monitor how long your group has for discussion time and answer as many of these questions together as you can.

READING

Turn back to the list of "Grace is" statements in the reading (see page 164). Let each group member say which one most stood out to them and why.

BIBLE STUDY

Look up the story of Paul's encounter with Jesus in Acts 9:1–23. Compare and contrast this narrative with Paul's own telling of the story in Acts 26.

PRAYER

As you prayed about your role in proclaiming the gospel, what ideas came to mind? What grace has God given you for preaching to certain others?

ACTION

Discuss the ethnic, national, cultural, political, socioeconomic, and gender differents represented in your group. How are you different from each other? How are you the same? In your group meetings, how have you felt or not felt God's Yes from each other? What do you need grace to do in your group to help you feel more comfortable with each other?

REFLECTION

For those who are willing, read some ideas from your journals to each other. Who do you struggle to connect with? Be kind in the way you speak, realizing that people groups you think negatively about could be represented in your group.

GROUP PRAYER

Hold hands as you pray. Whoever would like to pray out loud can take turns praying for all of you to grow in grace and love for each other so your unity will deepen.

As your group meeting ends, pray the Lord's Prayer together:

> *Our Father in heaven, hallowed be your name, your kingdom come, your will be done, on earth as it is in heaven. Give us today our daily bread. And forgive us our debts, as we also have forgiven our debtors. And lead us not into temptation, but deliver us from the evil one, for yours is the kingdom and the power and the glory forever. Amen. (Matthew 6:9–13)*

REST

Plan a fun activity with someone who is different from you. Go out and experience an interest you share in common. Commit to not talk about anything stressful or contentious but just enjoy each other's company.

LESSON 20

LOVE

▪ PERSONAL STUDY ▪

READING

As you begin your discipleship time today, say the Jesus Creed out loud:

Hear, O Israel, the Lord our God, the Lord is one. Love the Lord your God with all your heart, with all your soul, with all your mind, and with all your strength. The second is this: love your neighbor as yourself. There is no commandment greater than these.

For Paul, love is central. It was central because he knew the challenges of the Christian life for those who were in fellowship with one another in house churches dotting the Roman Empire. The only way they would make it is if each person learned to love the others. Roman slaves and workshop owners were not used to sitting down at a table and praying with Torah-observant Jews, and kosher Jews were not used to reading Scripture with prostitutes or migrant workers—yet Paul believed this was God's greatest vision for living! Which brings us back to the need to love one another.

LOVE IS A GREAT IDEA UNTIL . . .

Love is a great idea until the one you are called to love happens to be unlike you. Love is a great idea until you discover who your neighbors actually are. . . . Love is a great idea until your kids go ballistic. Love is a great idea until your house floods because someone left the sink running. Love is a great idea until you see who sits next to you at church on Sunday morning. (Page 52, FOD)

BUT WHAT EXACTLY IS LOVE?

Define love in the Bible by watching God love Israel, his Son, and the church—in fact, the whole of creation. God shows us what love is, and we can't answer our question until we turn away from the dictionary's emphasis on emotions and affections and go to the Bible's special way of revealing what love is. . . .

Our culture defines love by emotional experience, by pleasure, and by satisfaction . . .

Because our culture—and many Christians—are so enculturated into this sense of love, we struggle with love in our marriages, in our families, and in our relationships with close friends and with one another in what should be our salad bowl churches. Why do we struggle? Because we've got our hearts wrapped around the wrong ideas about love. Does the Bible's sense of love begin with dopamine bliss? No. It begins in a spot most in our culture want to ignore, so let's turn now to the first of four elements of love in the Bible. (Page 53, FOD)

Element 1: Rugged Commitment

The Bible begins telling us what love is with the thoroughly unexciting idea of God making a covenant commitment with Abraham. (Read Genesis 12 and 15.) . . . a covenant commitment that finds new expression in the promise to David, discovers a brand new future in the new covenant prophecy of Jeremiah 31, and then lands on the final covenant God makes with us in Jesus Christ (what we call his "new covenant"). Love then is not primarily emotion or affection, but rather a covenant commitment to another person. Commitment does not deny emotions; commitment reorders emotions. (Page 53, FOD)

Element 2: Rugged Commitment to Be "With"

God's central covenant promise was that he would be with Israel: "I will be your God, and you will be my people." How was God with humans? . . . As the Bible unfolds, God expresses his presence with Israel in a pillar of cloud and fire, then in a mobile shrine called a "tabernacle," and then in a huge, immobile temple. . . . But God's deepest commitment to be "with" was expressed through the incarnation. . . . Jesus was "Immanuel . . . God with us" (Matthew 1:23), and this theme of with-ness continues: Jesus, after his resurrection, sends the Spirit to be with us. . . . God's covenant is a commitment to be with us. (Pages 53–55, FOD)

Love is a rugged commitment by one person—married or not—to another person . . . The relationship may weather stormy waters, but love hangs on through the storm. It is the hanging on . . . that illustrates what love is. Person A says to Person B, "I'm here with you through it all." (Page 57, FOD)

Element 3: Rugged Commitment to Be "For"

Love in the Bible is also a rugged commitment to be for a person. To love someone means you are their advocate, on their side. (Page 57, FOD)

God's rugged commitment is to be with us and for us. God's for-ness is something that is expressed over and over in the Old Testament covenant formula, "I will be their God and they will be my people." We could translate this as "I've got your back" or "I'm on your side" or "I'm with you as the God who is for you." . . . God's love is a covenant of supporting strength; he is our proponent; he is our advocate. He's on our side. (Page 58, FOD)

Element 4: Rugged Commitment "Unto"

We learn love by watching God, who loves in a rugged covenant commitment to be with us, to be for us, and—here is the fourth element of love—unto his perfect design for us.

If "with" is the principle of presence and "for" the principle of advocacy, unto-ness is the principle of direction. God loves us, and God's kind of love transforms us into loving and holy, God-glorifying and other-oriented people in God's kingdom. God's with-ness transcends simple presence and advocacy; his with-ness and for-ness are a transforming power. . . .

Genuine friendships, which are two-way, are always transformative. One reason, then, we don't love those unlike us in the church is because we don't want their presence rubbing off on us, or because we can't control our influence on them. (Page 59, FOD)

. . . to love a person means we are committed to being with them, to our presence with them. To love a person also means they know that we are for them; they need to know our hand is on them and behind them. And to love a person means that together in our mutual indwelling we strive unto kingdom realities, or Christlikeness, or holiness, or love, or full maturity in Christ. (Page 61, FOD)

Reflection questions on the reading

1. What does the reading say are the four aspects of biblical love?

2. In what ways does the reading challenge or affect your view of "love"?

3. Based on this definition of love and on honest self-examination, who are some people you truly love? Who shows this kind of love to you?

BIBLE STUDY

Jesus' Example of Love (John 13)

Jesus is the "exact representation of [God's] being," (Hebrews 1:3) so Jesus was able to provide a living example of God's rugged commitment to be with us, to be for us, and to transform us. In this chapter, John tells a first-person account of the night before his friend Jesus died.

Read John 13:1–35.

1. Write down all the references to love in this chapter. What picture does this give you of Jesus' type of love?

2. How do you see Jesus being *with* his friends?

3. How do you see Jesus being *for* his friends?

4. How do you see Jesus encouraging transformation *unto* godliness in his friends?

PRAYER

Make time to be *with* God. Set aside at least thirty minutes when you can be alone. If you prefer silence, create a quiet environment. If music helps you connect with God, play worship music of your favorite style. Choose a position that will help you focus on God. If you are physically able, consider lying facedown on the ground. Lying prostrate like this can be a symbol of our surrender or adoration. You could also kneel or sit with your palms open and facing upward. Try to let go of distractions and invite God to be present with you by the Holy Spirit. You are trying to consciously be *with* God—and remember that God wants to be *with* you too.

As you conclude your prayer time, pray the Lord's Prayer:

> *Our Father in heaven, hallowed be your name, your kingdom come, your will be done, on earth as it is in heaven. Give us today our daily bread. And forgive us our debts, as we also have forgiven our debtors. And lead us not into temptation, but deliver us from the evil one, for yours is the kingdom and the power and the glory forever. Amen. (Matthew 6:9–13)*

ACTION

- Think of a friend who needs support or an advocate or encouragement. What could you do to show that you are *for* them? Go and do that to show your love.

REFLECTION

- Have you ever told yourself that you were doing something out of love for someone, but you realized your actions weren't actually loving? Has someone ever said hurtful words to you while claiming they were simply "speaking the truth in love"? Think about why presence and advocacy are so important in showing love before we try to point people in a direction of growth. Journal your thoughts and experiences of authentic versus inauthentic love.

▪ GROUP DISCUSSION ▪

When your group meeting begins, say the Jesus Creed together:

Hear, O Israel, the Lord our God, the Lord is one. Love the Lord your God with all your heart, with all your soul, with all your mind, and with all your strength. The second is this: love your neighbor as yourself. There is no commandment greater than these.

The following questions are based on the personal study you already have completed. Monitor how long your group has for discussion time and answer as many of these questions together as you can.

READING

▪ Share stories of real love you have experienced, seen, or heard about.

▪ Who has made you feel really loved in your life?

BIBLE STUDY

▪ How does Jesus show God's rugged commitment to love people?

▪ Do you think the disciples felt like Jesus loved them? Why or why not?

PRAYER

Did you sense in any way God's presence with you as you prayed? What was that like? If you did not, is waiting for God's presence something you want to try again?

ACTION

1. The reading talked about our struggle with loving others who are different because we don't want to be like them or feel like we can't influence them to become like us. Think of someone you know who is different from you whom you have a hard time loving with biblical commitment. Discuss this with your group (being careful not to put down the people you're talking about). Take time to each write a note to someone who is different from you, expressing in some way your rugged commitment to be with them and for them.

2. If your meeting space will allow for this, get a bowl of warm water and a towel. Take turns washing each other's feet. This is a foreign concept in modern American culture, so it may feel awkward. As you literally follow Jesus' example in foot washing, think about how you can literally follow his example of loving others like he commanded.

REFLECTION

Share with each other some ways you wish people would demonstrate their with-ness and for-ness with you. What are your needs for love in your life, and how could your group members help you feel authentically loved?

GROUP PRAYER

Just as you asked God to be present with you alone, now ask God to be present with your group. Sit in silence or listen to music for 10–15 minutes.

As your group meeting ends, pray the Lord's Prayer together:

> *Our Father in heaven, hallowed be your name, your kingdom come, your will be done, on earth as it is in heaven. Give us today our daily bread. And forgive us our debts, as we also have forgiven our debtors. And lead us not into temptation, but deliver us from the evil one, for yours is the kingdom and the power and the glory forever. Amen. (Matthew 6:9–13)*

REST

Calming racing thoughts and busy schedules to make time to connect with God can be a challenge, but it can be refreshing. As you rest after this study, make more time to be alone with God and invite God to be present with you as you rest.

21

LESSON 21

TABLE

> **Learning intent:** Disciples will learn about life in the first-century church and their practices of Table fellowship.
>
> **Spiritual formation intent:** Disciples will look at the context of some of Paul's teachings in his letters and consider how we can apply those principles in our different culture today.

■ PERSONAL STUDY ■

Reading

As you begin your discipleship time today, say the Jesus Creed out loud:

Hear, O Israel, the Lord our God, the Lord is one. Love the Lord your God with all your heart, with all your soul, with all your mind, and with all your strength. The second is this: love your neighbor as yourself. There is no commandment greater than these.

Imagine "going to church" in the first century. If you were in a major Roman city, such as Rome, Ephesus, or Pompeii, you'd leave your home and walk in your leather sandals (or barefoot) through the city on paved roads. The pavers in your city are large stone blocks, not as smooth or as square as the ones we find in our driveways or walkways today, and it is hard not to stub your toe or trip.

You enter a house church where everyone gathers, and you immediately encounter some "church kids" playing hide-and-seek; someone's slave passes you carrying a spit with some already roasted meat dangling on the end. You also see that the household's former shrine to Apollo has been desecrated—better yet, liberated from idols. You walk through an atrium, where the evening sun gently falls on you, and then a few steps beyond the atrium you enter into a large room where others are sitting. Some lounge on the floor while others are on sofas with pillows. Someone—a slave—is fanning what appears to be an important leader. It is the "elder" (what we call "pastor" or "priest"), who has a small scroll open, and he's chatting with someone about what it says.

Outside the room on the veranda are low tables, and some have already taken their seats for dinner. There are flasks of wine and some pots of water and some trays of food—chicken and fish—and some "veggies" and some baked bread. There you sit at the table, eating next to a Roman magistrate whom you had not met other than in a legal case some time back, but he doesn't remember you. He does "pass the peace," however, with a handshake and a kiss to the cheek. You also meet a young Jewish man who not only follows the Torah, but believes in Jesus, and you observe that he's eating what he calls "kosher."

Across the room, you observe that a slave, instead of serving others, is sitting next to a Roman citizen, their different statuses identified by their clothing, and they are praying together with their hands clasped. The conversation is going wonderfully with others around you when someone— the elder—stands up and says a prayer to lead the group into the Eucharist. The elder reads from the great apostle who had been to this city some years back, and what he reads about is Jesus' betrayal and death and the resurrection to the throne of God. You hear about bread and body and about wine and blood, and then he passes bread and wine around the room.

You snap off some bread, eat it, and then take a deep gulp of wine. You pass these to the magistrate next to you, and the table grows silent. Your thoughts wander to what has happened to you because of what happened to Jesus—dying so that you now are saved from a life of sin. You recall your own liberation as you sit with a few dozen liberated people. Your world has been turned upside down, your husband tolerates your "superstition," your oldest son thinks you're stupid, while your daughter and younger son sometimes accompany you. You hope your husband will join you too someday, and you have begun to notice an urgency in your prayers for your eldest son, sometimes moving into tears or anxiety. He's becoming far too Roman in his ways, and you know Roman ways lead to slavery to sin and grasping for status and uninhibited sexual expression.

The elder speaks about the cup and announces it is God's love and grace and Yes for everyone. He reports a sad story he heard about a church in Greece (you thought he was referring to Corinth but he didn't mention the city), where some of the wealthier followers of Jesus were eating before the poorer ones arrived. The elder makes it clear that Roman ways stop at the door, and that everyone, men and women, slaves and free, Jews and Greeks, and rich and poor are all one family in Christ. The elder then says this Passover-meal cup is a cup of thanksgiving (*eucharistia*), and that by drinking from that cup each person is participating in the death of Jesus, the Jewish Messiah who can liberate the Romans, and you realize how personal this is to you. He then says that eating the bread means you have just partaken in the body Jesus gave for us, a body that made you all one, whether you are Jewish or Roman, man or woman, a slave or a Roman citizen (which you are).

The elder then warns about dancing with the demons by engaging in worship in the Roman shrines. Your husband keeps one in your own residence near the front door, and previously the elder spoke with you about the host's conversion and how he tore down and destroyed the shrine to Apollo in this home. The elder urged you to be very, very careful about eating food offered to idols because the host was still struggling with his commitment to Jesus as the one true Lord.

As the sun is fading over the Italian countryside . . . you prayed for God's good hand of grace to fall on your family as it had fallen on you. Throughout the evening, the elder has connected the whole of life to the Eucharist because the church begins at that table. What you experience in the villa is an amazing fellowship, a new kind of family. . . .

Ordinary Romans now in Christ would have been struck by how equal everyone was in such a setting. (Pages 96–98, FOD)

Reflection questions on the reading

1. What surprised you most in this description of a first-century house church?

2. If you had lived during that time period, where do you think you would fit in a house church meeting? Would you be a slave, a tradesperson, a wealthy elite? Where would you fit in the religious/ethnic/socioeconomic mix of that fellowship of differents?

3. How does this early church meeting sound different from modern church services? How is it the same?

BIBLE STUDY

Paul's Table (1 Corinthians 10–11)

Paul wrote these instructions to the house churches in Corinth about coming to the table together.

Read 1 Corinthians 10:14–33.

1. What are the problems in the churches in Corinth that Paul is addressing? What instructions does he give them?

2. Paul tells them in verse 24 to seek the good of others instead of their own good. In verse 33, he shows that he takes his own advice. *Why* does he say he seeks the good of others?

3. Most Americans don't have to deal with matters of conscience about eating meat sacrificed to idols. What matters of conscience about eating and drinking do you face today? How can Paul's advice to the Corinthians give you wisdom for today?

Read 1 Corinthians 11:17–28.

4. What are the problems in the churches in Corinth that Paul is addressing? What does Paul tell them they should do differently?

5. What principles from Paul's advice can apply to you as you approach the table of the Lord's Supper?

6. As you read the Bible passages after having read the selection from *A Fellowship of Differents* about the early church, did the Scriptures seem alive to you in a new way? If yes, how?

PRAYER

Paul encouraged the Corinthian followers of King Jesus to examine themselves before they approached the table. He specifically talked about their greed and selfishness regarding the poor among them. As you pray today, ask God to help you examine yourself. What divisions between you and other Christians exist in your heart? What greed or selfishness or mistreatment of the poor do you find in yourself?

As you conclude your prayer time, pray the Lord's Prayer:

> *Our Father in heaven, hallowed be your name, your kingdom come, your will be done, on earth as it is in heaven. Give us today our daily bread. And forgive us our debts, as we also have forgiven our debtors. And lead us not into temptation, but deliver us from the evil one, for yours is the kingdom and the power and the glory forever. Amen. (Matthew 6:9–13)*

ACTION

How can you share a meal with hungry people in your community? Find a food bank or organization that provides meals and ask them what they need. Go grocery shopping for them.

REFLECTION

▪ Paul gave very specific instructions to believers in Corinth to help them approach their specific fellowship problems in a way that would honor God. What timeless principles do you see in the Bible study passages that could help you honor God today in your culture?

■ GROUP DISCUSSION ■

When your group meeting begins, say the Jesus Creed together:

Hear, O Israel, the Lord our God, the Lord is one. Love the Lord your God with all your heart, with all your soul, with all your mind, and with all your strength. The second is this: love your neighbor as yourself. There is no commandment greater than these.

The following questions are based on the personal study you already have completed. Monitor how long your group has for discussion time and answer as many of these questions together as you can.

READING

■ Discuss with the group the meetings that you have had together over the past months. What moments have you shared that remind you of the meeting of the first-century church?

BIBLE STUDY

■ If you have spent much time in church, how have you seen the Lord's Supper observed? How often? In what style?

■ Have you heard church leaders read from 1 Corinthians 11:23–26 during a Communion service? Did they ever explain the bigger context of Paul's instructions?

■ How does reading those verses in their context help you better understand Paul's words about the tradition of the Lord's Supper?

PRAYER

If you are willing, share anything that God convicted you about as you prayed and examined yourself.

ACTION

1. As the first-century church often shared meals and came to the Table together, if your denominational tradition allows for you to celebrate Communion without a clergy person to bless the bread and wine, and if you are all comfortable with it, come to the Table together with your group and share a meal and celebrate Communion. Someone can bring bread and wine or grape juice. Have someone read 1 Corinthians 11:23–26 out loud as you remember King Jesus together.
2. If you prefer not to share in Communion as a group, then at least plan to have a meal together.

REFLECTION

As you journaled, what ideas did you have about how you can work out Paul's advice for unity and sharing in your lives today?

GROUP PRAYER

Let each group member pray out loud about a division they see in the global or local church today. Pray for unity among all God's people.

As your group meeting ends, pray the Lord's Prayer together:

> *Our Father in heaven, hallowed be your name, your kingdom come, your will be done, on earth as it is in heaven. Give us today our daily bread. And forgive us our debts, as we also have forgiven our debtors. And lead us not into temptation, but deliver us from the evil one, for yours is the kingdom and the power and the glory forever. Amen. (Matthew 6:9–13)*

REST

Proper sleep is a key part of rest and health. Make time in your schedule to get a full night's sleep. If you struggle with a sleep disorder or mental or physical health complications with your sleep, is there any step you can take to work toward solutions? This isn't to shame you or make you feel bad—just to remind you that rest matters to God, and it's okay to spend time in your discipleship process to get healthy. If you would like to read some verses on sleep, see Psalm 3:5, Psalm 4:8, and Proverbs 3:24.

22

LESSON 22

HOLINESS

> **Learning intent:** Disciples will learn that holiness means being set apart and devoted to God's special use.
>
> **Spiritual formation intent:** Disciples will open themselves up to the Holy Spirit's transforming work to make them holy.

■ PERSONAL STUDY ■

READING

As you begin your discipleship time today, say the Jesus Creed out loud:

Hear, O Israel, the Lord our God, the Lord is one. Love the Lord your God with all your heart, with all your soul, with all your mind, and with all your strength. The second is this: love your neighbor as yourself. There is no commandment greater than these.

> For the Torah-devout Jewish apostle Paul, leaning as he was every day into a mission to the (demonstrably sinful) gentiles and the (not quite as demonstrably sinful) Jews, holiness was the air he breathed and the challenge he saw for the churches. There wasn't a day that he was not aware of the opportunity for each of his churches for a life devoted to God. The Bible's big idea about holiness comes to expression in Leviticus 11:44–45: "I am the LORD your God; consecrate yourselves and be holy, because I am holy. Do not make yourselves unclean by any creature that moves along the ground. I am the LORD, who brought you up out of Egypt to be your God; therefore be holy, because I am holy."
>
> Here we see the two major elements of holiness in the Bible:

1. God is holy.
2. Therefore, God's people are to be holy.

Our holiness is grounded in God's prior holiness, which means we have to figure out what it means to be holy in this messed-up fellowship called the church. No one experienced the challenge of holiness more than the apostle Paul, because those Roman Empire house churches were filled with folks who didn't have a clue what "holiness" meant. (Pages 115–16, FOD)

If God *is* holy, and if God is *prior to all creation*, and if some say holiness means being different from or separate from something or someone else, *when God was "all alone" and there was nothing else, was God holy then*? Yes, in fact, God was and is and always will be holy. This leads us to an important point: holiness cannot be reduced to separation or difference. At a deeper level, holiness means "devoted." In the Do's and Don'ts approach, holiness should focus on the Do's. In other words, if separation focuses on differences from the world, the deeper level of devotion focuses on a life devoted unto God. The two belong together, and we need both. (Page 117, FOD)

There are three elements to holiness. First, we don't make ourselves holy; holiness is the inner work of God. Second, holiness means learning to live a life that avoids sins. Third, holiness means learning to live a life devoted to God. We'll combine the second and third because Paul does so often. (Pages 117–19, FOD)

The apostle Paul points us directly to the spring of the spiritual life, and *it is the work of God's Spirit in us that produces holiness*. Let me quote a few lines from Paul to make this abundantly clear, and I have italicized those words that draw our attention to God as the source of holiness:

"May God *himself*, the God of peace, *sanctify* you through and through."

(1 Thessalonians 5:23)

". . . because God chose you as first fruits to be saved through the *sanctifying work of the Spirit* and through belief in the truth.

(2 Thessalonians 2:13)

From Paul's earliest letters to some of his latest, the theme remains the same: holiness is the work of God in us. So if we want our church to become holy, we need to learn to spend time in God's presence, basking in the light of his holiness. (Page 119, FOD)

God wants us not to do some behaviors, and God wants other behaviors to mark his people. But because holiness is about devotion, it is best not to talk about "Do's and Don'ts," but rather about "Don'ts because of the Do's." That is, because we are doing devotion to God, we don't want to do sin. (Page 120, FOD)

I can think of no passage in the Bible that teaches holiness better than Ephesians 4 and 5, which we could call Paul's version of the "Don'ts because of the Do's." In this passage we have to imagine Paul's house churches filled with shop workers, slaves, migrant workers, and males struggling with what they were learning in the church. Paul wanted the churches to be holy, and that for him meant a life devoted to God. But Paul did not begin the Christian life with a list of Don'ts. He began it with a vision for each of us to be fully devoted to God. (Page 120, FOD)

Reflection questions on the reading

1. Have you thought much before about the word "holiness"? Before doing this reading, how would you have defined holiness?

2. What strikes you as the difference between focusing on avoiding sin (being set apart) and focusing on being devoted to God?

3. What does the reading say is the source of holiness in the life of Jesus-followers? How does a transformation into holiness work?

BIBLE STUDY

Holiness Do's and Don'ts (Ephesians 4–5)

Let's look at what Paul tells the Christians in Ephesus that they should do and should not do in order to become holy.

Read Ephesians 4:1–4 and 4:14–32.
Read Ephesians 5:1–20.

1. Divide the space below into two columns: DO and DON'T. Go through the verses listed above and write down every instruction under one of those two columns.

PRAYER

Go back to the list you made during your Bible study. Select one DO and one DON'T that you have trouble with in your life. Pray and ask the Holy Spirit to come with transforming power into your life to help you be both set apart and devoted.

As you conclude your prayer time, pray the Lord's Prayer:

> *Our Father in heaven, hallowed be your name, your kingdom come, your will be done, on earth as it is in heaven. Give us today our daily bread. And forgive us our debts, as we also have forgiven our debtors. And lead us not into temptation, but deliver us from the evil one, for yours is the kingdom and the power and the glory forever. Amen. (Matthew 6:9–13)*

ACTION

Think of one of the DON'Ts that you have failed to practice. Have you lied, been destructive in your anger, stolen something, hurt someone with your words, been greedy? Or something else from your list above? Today, do what you need to do to confess this and make it right. A full and sincere apology may be enough, or you may need to make restitution of some kind. Take a step toward holiness by reconciling this.

REFLECTION

- Do you struggle more with the DO list or the DON'T list? Do you tend to sin more by commission (doing something actively wrong) or do you sin more by omission (failing to do something right)? What are your biggest battles for holiness? Journal about this.

■ GROUP DISCUSSION ■

When your group meeting begins, say the Jesus Creed together:

Hear, O Israel, the Lord our God, the Lord is one. Love the Lord your God with all your heart, with all your soul, with all your mind, and with all your strength. The second is this: love your neighbor as yourself. There is no commandment greater than these.

The following questions are based on the personal study you already have completed. Monitor how long your group has for discussion time and answer as many of these questions together as you can.

READING

- How does the holiness or lack of holiness of the individual members of a church affect that church's unity?

- How would it transform your church or your group of believers if you all grew in holiness? (Don't just point fingers at others—consider your own contributions to this as well!)

BIBLE STUDY

- Were any of the DO or DON'T instructions new to you?

- What do you think about considering holiness as much a matter of what we do as of what we should avoid?

PRAYER

If you are willing, share how you struggle with holiness. Also share if you feel like the Holy Spirit has been working to transform you in that area.

ACTION

A committed golfer wouldn't use a special golf club to hammer a nail. Having a special tool for a special purpose is an example of the "set apart" aspect of holiness. Before your group meets, see if someone in your group has a hobby that involves tools—anything from cooking to carpentry— and ask them to bring some samples to your group (the weirder, the better). Let other group members try to guess what each specialized tool does.

REFLECTION

How do you wrestle with sins of omission and sins of commission on your journey toward holiness? Author Jon Acuff wrote on his blog *Stuff Christians Like* about a concept called "The Gift of Going Second." He said that often in small groups, people confess "safe sins" like not reading the Bible enough. A courageous group member who is willing to go first and model vulnerability in confession gives all the other group members the gift of going second. Hopefully in the months of meeting together, the group has built safety and trust. If so, is one of you willing to go first and share your experiences with sin and holiness, making it easier for the others to speak up?

GROUP PRAYER

Pray gently and sincerely for each other to keep growing toward holiness as the Holy Spirit helps you become both set apart and devoted. Address the specific struggles the group members have shared.

As your group meeting ends, pray the Lord's Prayer together:

> *Our Father in heaven, hallowed be your name, your kingdom come, your will be done, on earth as it is in heaven. Give us today our daily bread. And forgive us our debts, as we also have forgiven our debtors. And lead us not into temptation, but deliver us from the evil one, for yours is the kingdom and the power and the glory forever. Amen. (Matthew 6:9–13)*

REST

Sometimes after sharing openly, people can experience anxiety or regret. Especially if you are feeling raw after your self-examination and group sharing this week, take time to do restful activities that build you up.

23

LESSON 23

NEWNESS

Learning intent: Disciples will learn ways that God's politics differ from the world's politics and look at four principles about a new way of political interaction from Paul's life and teaching.

Spiritual formation intent: Disciples will face the sometimes-uncomfortable topic of politics and look at ways they can focus their allegiance on God's kingdom rather than the world's political systems, through loving others and forming a new politics in the church.

 **PERSONAL STUDY**

READING

As you begin your discipleship time today, say the Jesus Creed out loud:

Hear, O Israel, the Lord our God, the Lord is one. Love the Lord your God with all your heart, with all your soul, with all your mind, and with all your strength. The second is this: love your neighbor as yourself. There is no commandment greater than these.

In Scot's book, *A Fellowship of Differents*, this excerpt discusses four types of newness in the Christian life that we can experience in the church: a new freedom, a new faithfulness, a new guidance, and a new politics. While all are important, this reading only addresses one, because it seems to be one of the biggest challenges to unity among differents: a new politics.

God's mission in this world is to create the church where God's will is lived out by all of God's people. God's new creation grace and love are experienced at the table of Christian fellowship and create a new people, a new community, and a new way of life marked by a holiness the Roman Empire either despised or had never seen embodied in a community. . . . God's mission in the church is God's kind of politics, but God's politics is not the world's politics . . .

Before we take one more step, we need to remind ourselves of this ultimate Christian truth: the final rule will be a theocracy. God will rule through King Jesus over the whole world. With that important reminder baptizing every political controversy and voting season, we ask, In the meantime, how do we live? (Page 180, FOD)

Paul was called by God into a ministry of getting Roman gentiles saved and working hard at getting saved gentiles to live in fellowship and peace with saved Jews. . . . Every element in Paul's plan raised the hopes and created worrying wonders in each of Paul's house churches. God's kind of politics begins with these elements:

1. There is one God (going against Rome's gods).
2. God is Israel's God made known in his Son, King Jesus, the Lord who saves both Jews and gentiles (this blasphemed the emperor's self-image and exalted status).
3. The true people of God, or ecclesia (church), are comprised of those who believe in Jesus and who live under his rule (this denied Rome's sense of privilege).
4. The way to live is to follow the Bible's teachings, from Torah to Jesus to the apostles' teachings (and this cut into the fabric of the Roman system of laws and culture). (Page 182, FOD)

I suggest we learn four principles from Paul:

BE GOOD CHRISTIAN PEOPLE IN THE EMPIRE

. . . When Paul speaks of Rome, he does so respectfully, and at some level he believed God's hand controlled even Rome (Romans 13:1–7). Paul's message clearly challenged the exalted claims of the powers of Rome, but he believed his followers were to constrain their freedoms (1 Corinthians 7:17–24) and pray for their rulers (1 Timothy 2:1–4). Perhaps we need a reminder that the ruler on the throne when Paul said this was none other than Nero . . . [who probably] was the one who killed both Peter and Paul. So Paul is praying then for his future murderer! (Page 183, FOD)

But for that first generation of Christians who sometimes experienced the rough side of the power's tongue and the sharp side of their swords, being a good citizen never meant doing whatever Caesar asked. Good citizenship is a posture of the one whose primary citizenship is under King Jesus. It is the posture of engagement for the sake of the kingdom, but it is never the posture of total obedience or subservience to Caesar. (Page 184, FOD)

RECOGNIZE THE STATE AS A TEMPORARY GOOD

In Romans 13:1–7, Paul affirms that God's providence includes rulers and states. In 2 Thessalonians 2:5–11, Paul speaks of God as the "restrainer" in the world. These two sections in Paul's letters lead to the conclusion that all state powers are temporary. . . .

But most of us know that this is just the starting point. What happens when we encounter [evil leaders]? At that point Paul's "good government" would no doubt be turned inside out to witness to the evil "principalities and powers" that corrupt God's designs. So our relationship to the state must be nothing less than "ambivalent." Yes, it's within God's design, but when it oppresses, the Christian cannot support the state. (Page 184, FOD)

CHALLENGE THE STATE WITH THE GOSPEL, EVEN IF IT MEANS RESISTANCE

The Christian may be a good citizen, but citizenship and patriotism or nationalism have limits. The Christian may see the state as good, but it is a temporary and not eternal good. Our politics are the "politics of Jesus," or the politics of God. Ultimately, God rules through King Jesus, and King Jesus' citizens live under him. The gospel message subverts any other message that lays claim to a person deeper than the claim of Jesus. To the degree that the state's claims are consistent with King Jesus' claims, the Christian is a good citizen. The moment the state lays claim beyond what Jesus claims, the Christian citizen is called to follow Jesus, regardless of what that means for one's life. (Page 185, FOD)

THE BEST WAY TO BE POLITICAL IS TO BE THE CHURCH

When Paul decided to focus on his fellowships with the word *church*, he chose a term that meant what kingdom meant for Jesus: God's new society.

This new creation fellowship, the church, is a profoundly political way of life, but it is a new kind of politics. We must be *political*—but we must do it by being profoundly *church*. The best Christian churches subvert the politics of the day . . . by creating a culture that brings the life of God for all. This salad bowl church, this fellowship of differents, is nothing less than a new way of being political.

This all draws to one point, and that is that the primary relation of the Christian to the state is to live under King Jesus in the church, the body of Christ, in such a way that we embody Christlikeness in a way that witnesses to the world. . . . In the new creation society, we find Romans getting along with Greeks, and Jews getting along with gentiles, men getting along with women, and slaves getting along with the free and powerful, and, yes, Democrats getting along with Republicans. Paul's political theory, in fact—God's kind of politics—is the church. (Page 187, FOD)

Reflection questions on the reading

1. What do you think about churches being "political," as far as mentioning government and political parties from the pulpit?

2. What does the reading say about God's politics?

3. Which of the four political principles from Paul is the hardest for you to accept and practice? Why?

BIBLE STUDY

Paul, the Roman Citizen (Acts 16)

Paul and some ministry partners traveled into what is now northern Greece, where they met Lydia, a businesswoman, who decided to follow Jesus and offered hospitality to Paul and his crew. While they were staying in Philippi, they had a run-in with the law.

Read Acts 16:16–40.

1. How does Paul interact with the authorities in the beginning of the story? In the middle? At the end?

2. How does Paul use his Roman citizenship?

3. Which of Paul's four principles from the reading do you see in action here?

PRAYER

Paul and Silas prayed and sang hymns when they were in a terrible situation. What circumstances in your life feel hard or even hopeless right now? Today, in the face of those circumstances, try singing or praying to God in the hopeful spirit of Silas and Paul.

As you conclude your prayer time, pray the Lord's Prayer:

> *Our Father in heaven, hallowed be your name, your kingdom come, your will be done, on earth as it is in heaven. Give us today our daily bread. And forgive us our debts, as we also have forgiven our debtors. And lead us not into temptation, but deliver us from the evil one, for yours is the kingdom and the power and the glory forever. Amen. (Matthew 6:9–13)*

ACTION

Search on YouTube or Spotify for the song "A King and a Kingdom" by Derek Webb and listen to it. How does the song's call to pledge our allegiance to King Jesus instead of to a flag or a country speak to you?

REFLECTION

Do you struggle to find unity with Christians who vote differently than you do? Do you possibly even consider people who vote differently than you to not actually be Christians, even if they claim they are?

■ How can the principles in the reading help you process God's politics versus this world's politics and learn to make space and unity for Christians who are different in the realm of politics? How can you live together with them under King Jesus in the church?

▪ GROUP DISCUSSION ▪

When your group meeting begins, say the Jesus Creed together:

Hear, O Israel, the Lord our God, the Lord is one. Love the Lord your God with all your heart, with all your soul, with all your mind, and with all your strength. The second is this: love your neighbor as yourself. There is no commandment greater than these.

The following questions are based on the personal study you already have completed. Monitor how long your group has for discussion time and answer as many of these questions together as you can.

READING

- If your group has built relationships strong enough to lovingly disagree, discuss your politics with each other. How do you vote? Why do you vote that way? Which principles of God's politics do you take into the voting booth with you? Listen with empathy to each other.

- If the group facilitator doesn't think the group is ready for or open to this kind of conversation, discuss Paul's advice to pray for governing authorities, especially in light of what we now know—that Paul was killed by the Romans. What does praying for authorities look like for you?

BIBLE STUDY

- How do you see Paul act in submission?

- How do you see Paul act in resistance?

PRAYER

▪ What circumstances are you trying to praise God in right now?

ACTION

What are the ways that governing authorities are working for good in your life? How can you be a good citizen? What are ways that governing authorities make claims that counter the ways of Jesus? What action can your group take to resist ungodly pressure your government places on you? Discuss and make a plan to do something.

REFLECTION

Share from your journals. What ideas did you come up with for building unity in the church in the face of differences?

GROUP PRAYER

Write a prayer need on a piece of paper—don't sign your name. Put them in a pile and shuffle them. Each person can then choose a paper and pray out loud for the request.

As your group meeting ends, pray the Lord's Prayer together:

> *Our Father in heaven, hallowed be your name, your kingdom come, your will be done, on earth as it is in heaven. Give us today our daily bread. And forgive us our debts, as we also have forgiven our debtors. And lead us not into temptation, but deliver us from the evil one, for yours is the kingdom and the power and the glory forever. Amen. (Matthew 6:9–13)*

REST

If you normally go to church on Sunday morning, consider skipping it. Sometimes "going to church" can become a rote routine or a burden. Take a Sunday off and really rest.

If you don't normally go to church, try going. See if the experience of worshipping God and learning together with people who follow the same King—even if you have other differences—feels restful to you.

24

LESSON 24

FLOURISHING

> **Learning intent:** Disciples will see how the Holy Spirit builds unity in the church through giving spiritual gifts to each member.
>
> **Spiritual formation intent:** Disciples will look at the gifts the Spirit has given them and consider how to use them to love and serve each other.

■ PERSONAL STUDY ■

READING

As you begin your discipleship time today, say the Jesus Creed out loud:

Hear, O Israel, the Lord our God, the Lord is one. Love the Lord your God with all your heart, with all your soul, with all your mind, and with all your strength. The second is this: love your neighbor as yourself. There is no commandment greater than these.

> All we need to flourish in God's grand experiment, the church, is the Spirit of God. All we need is God's power for what God wants to accomplish . . .
>
> Our ability, our hopes, our efforts, and our strategies are insufficient to bring us all into one body. Believing in the power of "our-ness" is why some gravitate to separate-but-equal churches and why others resort to uniformity-by-conformity churches. In one, there is no challenge to cross ethnic, cultural, and gender lines, while in the other you either agree or go home. Either way, we get "our" wishes. Twenty centuries of dismal disunity and the witness of a fractured church ought to convince us of our raw inability to be the church God wants us to be. The hope of this book is that history will be reversed by a renewed commitment to be the church God designed, a church

that flourishes in a salad bowl fellowship of differents. But there is gospel—resurrection and new creation—news here: the Spirit can take our abilities and transcend them, then take our inabilities and transform them into the gracious power of unity. To flourish, then, we need to be Holy Spirit people. The only way the church can be God's kind of church is through the power of the Spirit. Only the Spirit empowers us to transcend differences and to transform our preferences into love for others. (Pages 191–92, FOD)

EXPOSURE TO THE SPIRIT MAKES US BIGGER

How does the Spirit make us bigger? By assigning us a gift in the big, cosmic mission of God. Through the Spirit's gifts, we become participants, actors on the divine stage, people gifted by God with an assignment and responsibility in the church of God. We must also see the paradox here that God's gifts make us bigger by making us needier! How so? What we learn from the gifts is that God gives to us a gift, but he gives everyone else a gift too, so that we need one another if the body of Christ is to function well. (Page 204, FOD)

When the Spirit comes, the Spirit assigns everyone a responsibility in the church, and in so doing the Spirit takes us away from our selfishness and individual life and makes us bigger. We flourish in the big work of God in this world. The four lists of the spiritual gifts differ, leading me to the observation that *these are representative examples of the Spirit's assignments.* I respect those who have compared the lists and tallied them and come up with *the* list of about twenty spiritual gifts. I further respect that such folks are trying to get people to think which of the gifts they "have" in the church, for all Christians need to ponder God's assignment. But I'm afraid being preoccupied with this list sometimes gets things backwards. Instead of looking at the list and wondering which one is me, a better approach is to ask, "What is the Spirit gifting me to do in the fellowship?" The answer to that question is your "gift."

You and I are given an assignment that locates us in what our big God is doing in this world. If that doesn't make us bigger, I don't know what does! Becoming "bigger" in this way also takes on direction, because our gifts are *for [unto] the good and unity of the body of Christ.* In one of Paul's last letters, he said this with utter clarity, so I will quote Ephesians 4:12–13, and break it up to make it easier to see why God gives us the gifts. First, they are given to God's people as an assignment:

To [unto] equip his people for works of service . . .

Why? Notice how oriented toward the "we" of the church this is:

. . . so that the body of Christ [not just "I"] may be built up . . .

And now the final end of the gifts:

> ... until we all reach unity in the faith and in the knowledge of the Son of God and become mature, attaining to the whole measure of the fullness of Christ.
>
> This is the big plan of God, and the gifts make us bigger by plugging us into that plan. (Pages 205–6, FOD)

Reflection questions on the reading

1. What do we need so we can flourish in the church?

2. How do spiritual gifts make us "needier"?

3. What is God's point in giving each follower of Jesus spiritual gifts?

BIBLE STUDY

The Gifts (Ephesians 4; 1 Peter 4; Romans 12; 1 Corinthians 12)

These are the four lists of gifts the reading talked about. They are probably not meant to be a comprehensive inventory of all possible gifts, but rather a representative sample.

Read Ephesians 4:11–16.

1. List the spiritual gifts mentioned in the verses:

2. What do verses 15 and 16 say about love?

Read 1 Peter 4:8–11.

3. List the spiritual gifts mentioned in the verses:

4. What does verse 8 say about love?

Read 1 Corinthians 12:4–11 and 13:1–4.

5. List the spiritual gifts mentioned in the verses:

6. What does 13:1–4 say about love?

Read Romans 12:4–10.

7. List the spiritual gifts mentioned in the verses:

8. What do verses 9 and 10 say about love?

PRAYER

Pray for the Holy Spirit to fill you and give you gifts to help you serve others with love in the church.

— *As you conclude your prayer time, pray the Lord's Prayer:*

> *Our Father in heaven, hallowed be your name, your kingdom come, your will be done, on earth as it is in heaven. Give us today our daily bread. And forgive us our debts, as we also have forgiven our debtors. And lead us not into temptation, but deliver us from the evil one, for yours is the kingdom and the power and the glory forever. Amen. (Matthew 6:9–13)*

ACTION

☐ Dr. Derwin Grey is a former doctoral student of Scot's. He is a pastor and author who shares his earned wisdom about leading multiethnic churches. Read the *Christianity Today* summary of his book *The High-Definition Leader* and write down the points that most stand out to you about multiethnic ministry—salad done the Right Way. https://www.christianitytoday.com/edstetzer/2015/september/20-truths-from-high-definition-leader-by-derwin-gray.html

☐ Visit a church with a very different ethnic or cultural makeup than the one you normally attend. Briefly note your main impressions.

REFLECTION

☐ As you have gone through these six lessons on unity in the church, what stirred your heart with delight? What made you uncomfortable? What do you most need to change in yourself to better get along in the salad bowl? How will you approach church differently now?

▪ GROUP DISCUSSION ▪

When your group meeting begins, say the Jesus Creed together:

Hear, O Israel, the Lord our God, the Lord is one. Love the Lord your God with all your heart, with all your soul, with all your mind, and with all your strength. The second is this: love your neighbor as yourself. There is no commandment greater than these.

The following questions are based on the personal study you already have completed. Monitor how long your group has for discussion time and answer as many of these questions together as you can.

READING

▨ What are your hopes for your church as you finish this study?

▨ How will you participate in helping your church become more of a fellowship of differents?

BIBLE STUDY

Encourage each other by looking at the spiritual gifts you listed during your study time and pointing out the gifts and abilities you see in each other. Make sure to mention gifts for each person—don't leave anyone out.

PRAYER

As you prayed this week, what gifts did you discover in yourself? What are you passionate about doing to serve the church?

ACTION

Plan a potluck salad bar meal to complete the study. Assign each person in the group an ingredient to bring so that you are all necessary for the good of the whole.

REFLECTION

Share your delights and discomforts with each other.

GROUP PRAYER

Stand in a huddle to pray, with your arms around each other. Let each person pray for themselves, each other, your group, the church, and the world.

As your group meeting ends, pray the Lord's Prayer together:

> *Our Father in heaven, hallowed be your name, your kingdom come, your will be done, on earth as it is in heaven. Give us today our daily bread. And forgive us our debts, as we also have forgiven our debtors. And lead us not into temptation, but deliver us from the evil one, for yours is the kingdom and the power and the glory forever. Amen. (Matthew 6:9–13)*

REST

You're done! Celebrate a well-earned day off. Don't read anything, don't study anything, don't DO anything . . . just relax and rest!

HOW TO FACILITATE A SMALL GROUP STUDY OF *FOLLOWING KING JESUS*

FACILITATION

The facilitator's most important job is clear communication. Let people know where to be and when and what to do when they get there. All throughout your group meetings, you will function as the guide. Lead them through the discussion time by asking the questions in the workbook, but enjoy the freedom to deviate from the suggested questions. If someone brings up an interesting point that the group wants to explore, guide them into and through it.

Keep track of the time. If you've told the group your meetings will be two hours long, keep your commitment. Officially end the meeting on time, and then offer (if it's okay with the host) to stay and keep talking with those who want to stay. That way, those who need to leave can do so without feeling bad.

Draw people out. If a group member doesn't usually answer questions, call them by name and ask their opinion. Let silence hang after you ask a question to allow people to think and to let quieter people gather their words to speak.

Guard the safety and confidentiality of your group members. If one group member starts to verbally attack or insult another, step in and stop it. Set clear guidelines when you begin for how you expect people to speak and behave during the discussions, and remind them of the guidelines if they violate them. Tell your group members that you will keep what they share only within your group, and you expect them to do the same for the others. The exception to this is if you are concerned a group member may be a danger to themselves or to someone else. More about that in the below section on pastoral care.

Read through the entire discussion guide for the week's lesson several days before your meeting. Some of the activities will require you to prepare. You will get to know your group. Sometimes you'll need to make judgment calls on which activities will go well with your group and which won't, and which discussion questions you might want to skip.

Clearly communicate every step of the way. Enjoy watching your group grow in relationship with God and each other.

HOSPITALITY

The group facilitator and the group host can be the same person but don't have to be. Does someone in your group have a living space big enough for your group and a willingness to host? Sharing responsibilities in the group can be good way for more people to get a chance to practice their spiritual gifts. Several group members could also take turns hosting.

Your group could meet at a restaurant or café, though keep in mind that some of the discussion topics can get personal, and some people aren't comfortable sharing in public places. If you meet at a café, be respectful of the space and the other patrons, order enough food and drinks to make it worth the business's time to host you, and tip really well.

Before the first meeting, send clear directions for the meeting place to all the group members. Don't just give them the address and expect them to rely on a GPS—make sure they get all the way to the right door. Include where to park and any parking costs, and tricky directions, and how to find the specific location, especially if you're meeting in a big apartment complex. A picture of the meeting place and a map can help. If anyone in your group has a disability or health problem that makes mobility difficult, make sure your meeting place can comfortably accommodate them.

Decide with your group if you will have meals together when you meet. A few of the group activities involve meals. Eating together can break down interpersonal barriers and help your group connect. A potluck meal offers opportunities for everyone to contribute. If you decide not to have meals together, try to at least offer some small snacks and drinks. The host can take responsibility for providing these, or the group members can share the work and take turns.

The most important role of the host is making people comfortable. Make sure they each feel individually welcomed. Provide enough seats for everyone. Let them know where the bathroom is (and make sure there is enough toilet paper!). A comfortable, safe environment will help people open up and share.

LEADERSHIP

Scot says that leadership gifts make themselves evident quickly. You may notice that one or more group members sets the tone for the group, inspires others, or shows an example that others follow. Or maybe someone is really good at explaining Bible passages or theological concepts in ways that other group members can understand. Consider asking those people to help you. They could take a turn facilitating the discussion or leading the prayer time.

If you notice other spiritual gifts, such as teaching or hospitality or mercy or helps, encourage people to use those gifts in the group. You lead well when you create an environment that helps others learn to lead also.

PASTORAL CARE

As the one who sees your group members every week and listens to them share about their lives, you will be one of the first people in their lives to notice problems. Be prepared to offer Jesus' kind of shepherding care to them. If a group member experiences a loss or tragedy, be there to comfort and support them. If they come to the group upset, it's okay to set aside your meeting agenda and just care for your friend as a group.

Do some reading about abuse, trauma, emotional health, and mental illness. You will have a chance to not only care for people's spirits but also for their emotions and bodies. Be prepared for the problems people may bring up in your group.

The exception to keeping confidentiality is when a group member says something that makes you think a crime has been committed or a person has been or could be harmed. If someone discloses abuse of a child or minor, you have an obligation to report this to the police. Don't take it to church leaders—go directly to civil authorities. If someone discloses abuse of an adult, try to talk with the victim and offer to help them report the abuse.

If someone makes statements that lead you to think they could be suicidal, such as, "I just want the pain to stop" or "I don't have any reason to keep living," ask follow-up questions. If they have an idea of how they might harm or kill themselves and a potential timeline, make sure they get to a psychiatrist for a mental health evaluation and suicide risk check. If they are in immediate risk of hurting themselves, take them to an emergency room.

You may be thinking, "Whoa, this is not what I expected in a discipleship workbook! Isn't this a little extreme?" I and the small group leaders I've trained have dealt with all of these situations. We weren't always well prepared, and we didn't always respond well. I've learned that it's vital for those who provide spiritual care to be ready to address mental and emotional health challenges as well. You don't need to be the one who has all the answers or who can adequately address all your group members' needs. But you may be the first one they open up to, so learn what resources are available in your community and help them get the professional care they need.

ACKNOWLEDGMENTS

Thank you to my husband, Matthew Miller, for working so hard to support my calling, and to our kids—Katherine, Joshua, Estel, Providence, and Iunia. I am grateful to Heather Culley, Rosie Roys, Abbie Daley, and my mom, Donna Castle, for helping Matthew and me care for our children and home while I wrote.

I loved working through the *Blue Parakeet* material with the DRx class on biblical interpretation and theology while I was creating this workbook. For your questions about the Bible, your enthusiasm, an abundance of baked goods, and all the laughter, thank you to Jessica Markink, Tom Gurbutt, Ashna Silas, Kayla Glewwe, Rosie Roys, Abbie Daley, Praveen Sam, Lucile Lesueur, Renske Letema, and our pastor, Matthew Lunders. Additional and immense thanks to Matthew for reading, discussing, editing, and improving the manuscript, and to my mom, Donna Castle, for helping Matthew and me care for our children and home while I wrote.

Thank you to the Maastricht Writers' Group for their ongoing friendship and support in their long-term investment in me as a writer.

Thank you to my professors at Northern Seminary who have also become my friends and mentors, Dr. Scot McKnight and Dr. Cherith Fee Nordling. The way you follow Jesus in your lives, teaching, speaking, and writing inspires me.

I am grateful to Scot for bringing me into this project and for going above and beyond to teach me about writing books and pastoring people. Thank you to John Raymond, our editor at Zondervan, for his passion for discipleship in the church and his vision for this workbook.

Thank you to the leaders at Damascus Road International Church for trusting me with many opportunities to learn about discipleship and small groups as we have served together.